FOG FACTS

FOG FACTS

Searching for Truth in the Land of Spin

Larry Beinhart

NATION
BOOKS

FOG FACTS
SEARCHING FOR TRUTH IN THE LAND OF SPIN

Published by
Nation Books
An Imprint of Avalon Publishing Group Inc.
245 West 17th St., 11th Floor
New York, NY 10011

AVALON
publishing group incorporated

First printing October 2005

Nation Books is a co-publishing venture of the Nation Institute and Avalon
Publishing Group.

Library of Congress Cataloging-in-Publication Data is available.

ISBN: 1-56025-767-9
ISBN 13: 978-1-56025-767-7

9 8 7 6 5 4 3 2 1

Book design by Maria Elias
Printed in the United States of America
Distributed by Publishers Group West

To Irving Beinhart
my father

To Gillian Farrell
my wife

The fiercest partisans of truth that I've ever met.

CONTENTS

Chapter One

THE FAILURE TO SEE WHAT'S BEFORE OUR EYES

———————

THE TRAGEDY OF 9/11 was a result of the failure to see the facts that were in front of us.

On April 1, 2001, Oklahoma State Trooper C. L. Parkins stopped one of the future hijackers, Nawaf Alhazmi, for speeding. Alhazmi had been photographed at an Al Qaeda meeting in Malaysia. He was known to the CIA as a terrorist. They suspected that he might be in the U.S. illegally. The CIA was, theoretically, looking for Alhazmi. Parkins ran Alhazmi's California license through the computer and checked for warrants. Nothing came back. The CIA had not distributed the information.

Trooper Parkins wrote Alhazmi two tickets totaling $138 and let him continue his journey.

Five months later, Nawaf Alhazmi would be one of the hijackers who took over American Airlines Flight 77.

That was just one of many instances in which 9/11 hijackers might have been picked up or kept out of the country or stopped before they boarded those planes in September.

This was not just a bureaucratic failure. By contrast, the 9/11 report offered "a reminder and an explanation of the one period in which the government as a whole seemed to be acting in concert to deal with terrorism—the last weeks of December, 1999, preceding the millennium." It was a time when information was not just "whispered about in highly classified intelligence dailies or FBI interview memos. The information was in all major newspapers and highlighted in network television news." The result was that "an alert Customs agent caught Ahmed Ressam bringing explosives across the Canadian border with the apparent intention of blowing up the Los Angeles airport. He was found to have confederates on both sides of the border."[1]

The idea of fog facts emerged from a series of very casual conversations I had between tennis games with Robert Brill, city desk editor at the Albany *Times Union*. I would get to the courts full of umbrage over something that I had discovered searching the Net that had not been reported in the mainstream media.

Rob would reply, almost invariably, "Oh, there was a story about that three months ago."

I would go home and do a search, and sure enough, the

1. *Report: The National Commission on Terrorist Attacks Upon the United States* (St. Martin's Press, 2004) pp. 214-215. As several critics have noted, the report works very hard not to point out that the Clinton administration made terrorism a priority and advocated openness in government while the Bush administration downgraded terrorism in its first year in office and chose secrecy whenever possible.

Times had indeed reported that Halliburton was being sued by its shareholders for the accounting practices instituted by Dick Cheney. On page 3 of the business section or something like that.

The things I was getting so worked up over were not secrets uncovered by political spies and underground agents of the next revolution. They were snippets picked up from the *Wall Street Journal*, CNN, and Fox News and now brought to my attention on a Web site. Even if they came from Greg Palast or Al Jazeera or the *Atlantic* or books by David Corn and Kevin Philips, they were all public facts. They were in print. They had been referred to, reviewed, and cross-referenced elsewhere.

Yet they seemed to be invisible.

I was working on a novel about an election like the one coming up in 2004. It seemed to me that the struggle to pull some of these facts out of the fog and make them important would be central to the real campaign. Therefore they had to be central to the campaign in the book, where it was described this way:

> . . . Fog Facts.
>
> That is, it was not a secret. It was known. But it was not known. That is, if you asked a knowledgeable journalist, or political analyst, or historian, they knew about it. If you yourself went and checked the record, you could find it out. But if you asked the man in the street if [the] president, who loved to have his picture taken among the troops and . . . aboard naval vessels, if you asked if he had found a way to evade service in Vietnam, they wouldn't have a clue and, unless they were against him already, they wouldn't believe it.

In the information age there is so much information that sorting and focus and giving the appropriate weight to anything has become incredibly difficult. Then some fact, or event, or factoid, mysteriously captures the world's attention, and there's a media frenzy. Like Clinton and Lewinsky. Like O.J. Simpson. And everybody in the world knows everything about it. On the flip side are the Fog Facts, important things that nobody seems able to focus on anymore than they can focus on a single droplet in the mist.

I live in the country. Sometimes the fog is so thick that you don't even know where you are. If you're driving, the beams from your headlights just bounce back at you. Then, as you go around a corner or the elevation changes, up or down, you emerge from the fog and suddenly everything is clear and you say to yourself, ah-hah, that's where we are.

This book is a journey somewhat like that. It's not a catalog of "fog facts." Nor is it a thesis. That they are caused by a single thing and this is what we should do to cure it. It touches on several issues, politics, the media, economics, the Bush administration, 9/11, and the 9/11 Report among them. A multitude of books have been written about each. Where that is the case, I saw no point in duplicating those fine efforts. Rather this is a journey in search of those moments where we come around the corner, or go down low, or rise up high, and see some particular thing or some series of events that allows us to say, "Oh, that's where we are."

• • •

There were many, many warnings about Al Qaeda, Osama bin Laden, and a terrorist strike inside the United States. They came from many sources, including Vladimir Putin, who said that there were suicide pilots training to attack us.[2]

The standard excuse, indeed the official excuse, for having ignored the warnings is that such attacks were unimaginable:

> I don't think anyone could have predicted that these people would take an airplane and slam it into the World Trade Center.

> National Security Adviser Condoleezza Rice,
> May 18, 2002

> Nobody in our government, at least, and I don't think the prior government, could envision flying airplanes into buildings on such a massive scale.

> President George Bush, April 18, 2002

That was not true.

Less than one year earlier, on October 24, 2000, the Pentagon had staged a mass casualty drill using the scenario of a hijacked airliner being flown into the Pentagon. Six months earlier, on March 4th, 2001, there had been a made-for-TV movie, the pilot for a Fox series called *The Lone Gunmen,* in which terrorists attempted to fly an airplane into the World Trade Center. In December 1994, Al Qaeda

---

2. www.foxnews.com/story/0,2933,53065,00.html, "Clues Alerted White House to Potential Attacks by Carl Cameron," Friday, May 17, 2002.

hijacked an Air France plane and attempted to fly it into the Eiffel Tower. On July 22, 2001, there were threats that Al Qaeda might attempt an air attack on a G8 summit in Genoa, Italy. The Italians closed the air space, kept fighters in the air and surrounded the conference with antiaircraft guns. Bush was present at that meeting and had to sleep on an aircraft carrier as a security measure, so it is reasonable to expect that he had some awareness of what was going on.[3] Yet these remained fog facts.

The 9/11 report said, "The most important failure was one of imagination."

Richard Posner, an appeals court judge who reviewed the report for the *New York Times*, said it revealed that:

> it is almost impossible to take effective action to prevent something that hasn't occurred previously. . . . The idea that [Al Qaeda] would [attack] by infiltrating operatives into this country to learn to fly commercial aircraft and then crash such aircraft into buildings was so grotesque that anyone who had proposed that we take costly measures to prevent such an event would have been considered a candidate for commitment.

Posner's conclusion offers a social and economic foundation for that failure of imagination. That certainly gets the

3. The Pentagon drill can be found at www.mdw.army.mil/news/ Contingency_Planning.html. *The Lone Gunmen* is out on DVD. You can find a description and clips at propagandamatrix.com/multimedia_ priorknowledge_lonegumen.html. The Air France hijacking can be found at www.pbs.org/wgbh/pages/frontline/shows/front/map/fr.html. The Genoa story is at archives.cnn.com/2001/WORLD/europe/07/17/ genoa.security/.

administration off the hook. But if he's correct, it means that we must always be fighting the last war and that useful foresight is impossible.

"Just the facts, ma'am," Sergeant Joe Friday used to say on *Dragnet*, the weekly TV show. Each episode, they told us, was taken from the actual files of the Los Angeles Police Department. A crime had been committed. The police came. They investigated. They found the facts. Those elemental, hard, and singular truths.

The criminal was arrested and tried and, invariably, convicted. Based on the facts. At the end of the show, they announced the sentence that had been handed down. Twenty-two minutes, and the world was returned to order.

After 9/11, with all the turmoil and panic, it was almost like that. In two days the White House announced that the gang was Al Qaeda and their leader was bin Laden. In two days the FBI announced the names of eighteen hijackers and a day later amended the list to add one more.

Facts are the light in the dark. The trail markers in the wilderness. They are what we need so as to go to the right places and do the right things.

It was reasonable, sensible, and logical to expect a full investigation. To get all the details of who and why and how. Including how such a disaster was possible and how it could be prevented.

At the same time, there was great resistance to an investigation.

All the relevant institutions of government, the intelligence services, the consulates and immigration, the FBI and the Federal Aviation Authority, even the military, had failed and didn't want their failures paraded in public.

The administration didn't want an investigation because the kindest thing that could be said about them was that they had been asleep at the wheel. Also, they knew where they wanted to go based on the 9/11 attacks. They wanted to go after Saddam Hussein. They knew that the facts of 9/11 would not support an invasion of Iraq. The facts would point to other places that the administration didn't particularly want to bother with. They might even point to Saudi Arabia, and the administration didn't want to go there at all.

Instead of a demonstration of how to pull the facts out of the fog, we had a demonstration of how a fog can be created. By foot-dragging, spinning, and quibbling. By hiding facts. By denying facts. By distortion and distraction. By waving the flag at nonexistent or irrelevant threats and going to war. By creating alternate narratives that are premised on things that didn't happen and obscure the things that did happen.

Still, the families of the victims fought for a committee of inquiry. They organized themselves and kept up relentless pressure. Their cause was so obviously sensible and so unarguably just and their moral authority so unquestionable that they could not be denied.

Two commissions were formed. There was the 9/11 Congressional Inquiry that was to look at just the failures in intelligence. Then there was the 9/11 Commission—the National Commission on Terrorist Attacks upon the United States—and they published a report. Benjamin DeMott in *Harper's Magazine* (October, 2004) describes it this way:

> [It] had to be the real thing. Some 2,500,000 pages of documents had been sifted, public testimony had been

taken from 160 different witnesses, 1,200 knowledge-
able persons interviewed in ten countries. . . . After
twenty long months working with a staff of close to
eighty, the ten Commissioners . . . [—] five Republicans,
five Democrats, ex-senators, governors, cabinet secre-
taries, big-time lawyers—had all signed on.

The title of DeMott's piece is "Whitewash as Public Service:
How the 9/11 Report Defrauds the Nation." His view is that
the report is one long alibi, that all its choices, its "voice," and
its overarching narrative are designed to say that the Bush
administration was not to blame.

The failure of the 9/11 report is much more basic than
that. It fails to do what Sergeant Joe Friday would have
done. Get "the facts, ma'am, just the facts."

Within two weeks of the FBI's publication of the names
and photographs of the nineteen hijackers, at least seven
seemed to have turned up alive elsewhere.

Saeed Alghamdi is a pilot in Tunisia, Salem Alhazmi is
working at a petrochemical plant in Saudi Arabia, Ahmed
Alnami is working as an administrative supervisor, and
Abduaziz Alomari is a pilot with Saudi Arabian Airlines.
According to the Saudi government, Mohand Alsheri is alive
and was not in the United States on September 11, 2001.

The brothers Waleed M and Wail M Alshehri are also
pilots and they are also alive, living in Saudi Arabia. Another
pair of brothers with the same names have disappeared. But
the two whose pictures appeared are alive and well.

The family of an eighth hijacker, Hamza Alghamidi,
says his photo "has no resemblance to him at all."

These reports come from the *New York Times*, the *Los
Angeles Times,* the BBC, the *Guardian,* the *Telegraph,* and

the *Independent* and are conveniently collated by the Center for Cooperative Research. The list, with more details, can be found on their Web site (www.cooperativeresearch.org) or in their book, *The Terror Timeline*.[4]

Yet the list as published in the 9/11 report still mentions those seven men among the nineteen hijackers. Neither does it debunk the reports that they are alive.

We do not even know the most basic facts of what happened on 9/11. They are lost in the fog. This time the fog is deliberate and manufactured.

4. Paul Thompson, *The Terror Timeline: Year by Year, Day by Day, Minute by Minute: A Comprehensive Chronicle of the Road to 9/11—and America's Response* (New York: Regan Books, 2004).

Chapter Two

LIES THAT BLIND US

———————

THE OFFICIAL AND still reigning story of America in these first years of the twenty-first century is that there was a sneak attack that could not be prevented, by a new force of evil in the world, terrorists. Like the fascists and the Communists, they have decided to enlist on the side of evil and they hate our way of life because its shining goodness threatens them as a flaming torch threatens the creatures that slink through the night.

Then George Bush rose to the occasion. He rallied the nation and struck back. He struck back where he thought the danger was the greatest, in Iraq. He thought that the Iraqis had weapons of mass destruction. He thought they were connected to the people who attacked us. After all, they were terrorists, Saddam Hussein ran a terrorist state, it was all one, like all those Communist states used to be, and all those Axis countries were. Fight one, you fight them all.

There are several great lies in there.

The most obvious ones and the most frequently refuted ones are that Iraq had WMDs and that Iraq was connected to Al Qaeda or to 9/11.

But there are others, perhaps more important, that are never addressed.

It is a lie that there are terrorists. At least in the sense that there are Christians, Moslems, Communists, Iraqis, and Americans.

Clearly there are people who commit acts of terror. There are people who have ideologies who use terror as a weapon. Lots of them. There are Chechnyan, Sikh, and Irish terrorists, leftist-anarchist Greek terrorists, there's Chakuku-Ha in Japan, the Armenian Secret Army for the Liberation of Armenia, the Tupac Katari Guerrilla Army in Bolivia, Puka Inti in Ecuador, and the Tamil Tigers in Sri Lanka. But there is no Terror for the Sake of Terror Army. There is no Movement to Change the World to a Terrorist Place.

The Department of Justice, during the eighties and nineties, classified domestic terrorists into six groups: Puerto Rican, Special Interest, Left Wing, Jewish Extremist, Anti-Castro Cuban, and Right Wing.

This was the hot terrorism story in 1981:

PUERTO RICAN TERRORISTS ALSO THREATEN
REAGAN ASSASSINATION[5]

Since 1975 . . . Puerto Rican terrorist groups have per-
petrated 260 acts of violence on the island, . . . from
bombings of banks, post offices and U.S. business enter-

---

5. Daniel James, "Puerto Rican Terrorists Also Threaten Reagan Assassination," *Human Events,* December 19, 1981.

prises to blowing up electric power plants and assaulting military installations and personnel. An estimated 70 or more violent attacks were committed on the mainland during the same period. The FALN[6] opened the "second front" with five bombings of prominent Manhattan locations, including the Rockefeller Center, on the very same day, October 26, 1974.

Mere weeks later, it killed a policeman in reprisal for the alleged murder of a Puerto Rican activist poet "by the racist New York Police Department."

Perhaps the FALN's most notorious act was the bombing of historic Fraunces Tavern in Lower Manhattan in January 1975, killing four and injuring more than 60 persons.

Imagine if we had hit San Juan with Shock and Awe.

Or, to follow the logic of this administration, if we had invaded Brazil. And rained bombs and missiles down upon Rio de Janeiro. And in the course of it, killed 20,000 to 100,000 Brazilians.

The way we responded to the Puerto Rican terrorists was with cops and prosecutors, just like on *Law and Order*. They were investigated, arrested, tried, and convicted. Some assuredly got away. Nonetheless, the Puerto Rican terrorist movement died down.

The second great lie that is never challenged is the War on Terror.

If we take "War on Terror" to be simple hyperbole, like the War on Poverty and the War on Drugs, meaning simply "great, maximum effort, with lots of publicity," that's fine.

6. Armed Forces of National Liberation.

But when we take it to mean actual invasions with lots of dead people who are irrelevant to the issue and the serious curtailment of our own civil rights and the employment of torture, then it's way over the top.

The lie that is necessary in order to tell all these other tales is that we could not have known about the 9/11 plot and we could not have stopped it. And this is a lie.

Should we have known? Yes, we should have. Could we have known? Yes.

Porter Goss, then-chairman of the House Permanent Select Committee on Intelligence and Republican co-chair of the Joint Intelligence Committee investigating 9/11, now director of the CIA

They don't have an excuse because the information was in their lap, and they didn't do anything to prevent it.

Senator Richard Shelby, ranking Republican on the Senate Intelligence Committee

I don't believe any longer that it's a matter of connecting the dots. I think they had a veritable blueprint, and we want to know why they didn't act on it.

Senator Arlen Specter, Republican member of the Joint Intelligence Committee Investigating 9/11

There were lots of warnings.

Secretary of Defense Donald Rumsfeld

If we could have known, utilizing the resources that were already in place, which were normal police and intelligence functions, and all we had to do was pay better attention, then that's all we have to do: pay better attention.

Instead of merely paying better attention we have had two wars with a few thousand of our people dead, over 100,000 Iraqis dead, some number of Afghans dead that has never been estimated or mentioned in public, the creation of a vast new homeland security bureaucracy, and serious incursions into our civil rights.

This has cost well over $200 billion. That's on top of all our normal defense and intelligence and criminal justice spending. Yet not a single one of the 9/11 backers, planners, or supporters has been brought to trial, convicted, and sentenced. As of March 13, 2005, "The 120 terrorism cases recorded on Findlaw . . . have resulted in only two actual terrorism convictions—both in a single case, that of Richard Reid, the notorious shoe bomber."[7]

Yet there are places where terrorists are arrested, tried and convicted.

FRANCE SENTENCES 6 TO PRISON TERMS IN 2001 PLOT

. . . for their role in a 2001 plot to attack the United States Embassy in Paris. . . .

The plot is one of three major Islamic terrorist operations that French intelligence and police officials have foiled in recent years—the others were an attack in Strasbourg in December 2000 and a plot in 2002 to

7. Karen J. Greenberg, "The Courts and the War on Terror," *Mother Jones* online, March 14, 2005, http://www.motherjones.com/news/dailymojo/2005/03/courts_war_on_terror.html

attack the Russian Embassy. . . . Fourteen people have been sentenced to prison in the Strasbourg plot. Those arrested in the Russian Embassy plot are awaiting trial.

New York Times, Wednesday, March 16, 2005

The "cheese-eating surrender monkeys," members of the "axis of weasels," have actually managed to catch, try, and convict twenty terrorists. More on the way.

They did this without invading Afghanistan or Iraq. Without endorsing new policies of torture, cutting back on civil rights, or bombing cities.

THE SACRED COW OF AFGHANISTAN

Even those who criticize the war in Iraq always, very quickly, add that of course the war in Afghanistan was good—we had to do that.

The primary reason we entered Afghanistan, we were told, was because they were harboring a specific felon, Osama bin Laden, plus a group of unnamed felons, his co-conspirators in the events of 9/11 as well as previous terrorist acts. We were going to get those people and shut down their operations.

We were, secondarily, there to oust the Taliban and to get their leader, Mullah Omar, technically for the offense of harboring this criminal gang and more generally because they were an oppressive, dangerous, fundamentalist Islamic government.

Bin Laden escaped.

It appears that almost all the major members of his gang escaped with him. An article in *USA Today* (March 2, 2003), "Al-Qaeda's Most Wanted: The Dead, the Captured and the At-Large," lists only one major Al Qaeda figure captured in Afghanistan and only three that were killed there, all of them by air strikes.

Although Afghanistan has had elections, and that's a wonderful thing, the country is generally in a state of chaos. Opium and heroin production have returned and are reaching record levels. The country is devolving rapidly toward being a narco-state. I would never argue that replacing an excessively moral religious government with drug gangs is a bad thing, but surely there must be somebody out there who thinks so. Why have we not heard their voices?

STATISTICS ON AL QAEDA KILLED AND CAPTURED

If the War on Terror is about getting the terrorists who attacked us in any way, shape, or form, surely we should know how we're doing. How many of them we've caught. What level they are. What they've done. How many are still out there.

Here's what our president has told us:

Some two thirds of Al Qaeda's key leaders have been captured or killed. The rest of them hear us breathing down their necks.

President George W. Bush, March 2, 2004

Which is about as specific as the administration has gotten. No one has ever said how many Al Qaeda members there were to begin with. So it's hard to say how many two thirds would be. We do know that few of the top leaders have been captured or killed.

In April 2004, a month after the president's "two thirds" statement, MSNBC published an "alive and at large" list of the top Al Qaeda leadership. There were forty-seven names on it. They included:

1. Osama bin Laden: The "emir" of Al Qaeda, the group's undisputed leader.
2. Ayman al-Zawahiri: The former head of Egyptian Islamic Jihad and an adviser and personal physician to bin Laden.
3. Saif Saif al-Din al-Ansari al-Adel: Al Qaeda's number three man, its military commander and chief military strategist. There is a reward of $25 million for information leading to his capture.
4. Amin al-Haq: Bin Laden's personal security coordinator.
5. Suleiman Abu Ghaith: Al Qaeda spokesman.
6. Mafouz Ould Walid: One of bin Laden's top aides.
7. Thirwat Saleh Shirhata: An Egyptian Islamic Jihad deputy emir, Zawahiri's number two. He has received two death sentences in absentia in Egypt for alleged terrorist activities. Believed to have been part of the plot to assassinate Anwar Sadat.
8. Abu Musab al-Zarqawi: Has ties to Al Qaeda, Al Ansar, and Hezbollah. He has participated in acts of terrorism, trained terrorists, led terrorist cells, and facilitated transport of terrorists and is being cited in the international press as a suspect in the recent devastating

bombing of the Jordanian embassy in Baghdad. The U.S. has established a reward of $25 million for information leading to his capture.

9. Mustafa Ahmed Hassan Hamza: Commander of the military branch of the Islamic Group. He was sentenced to death in absentia by an Egyptian court in the Returnees from Afghanistan case. It is believed he took part in the 1981 assassination of Egyptian President Anwar Sadat, the attempted assassination of President Mubarak in 1995, and the Luxor massacre, in which more than sixty German and Japanese tourists as well as Egyptian guides were killed, in 1997.

10. Fazul Abdullah Mohammed: Director of Al Qaeda operations in East Africa and a leading suspect in the November 28, 2002, terrorist attack on a beachfront hotel in Kenya who has been indicted by the FBI in connection with the August 6, 1998, bombing of the U.S. embassies in Nairobi, Nigeria, and Dar es Salaam, Tanzania.

11. Bilal bin Marwan: One of the oldest operatives in Al Qaeda, a senior lieutenant to bin Laden.

12. Mullah Omar: The Taliban leader who wouldn't hand over bin Laden and so precipitated the invasion of Afghanistan, is not on the MSNBC list. But, according to Fox News, he is still out there.[8]

On September 8, 2004, President Bush abruptly upped the estimate, saying that "more than three quarters of Al Qaeda's key members and associates have been detained or killed."

8. "Military Installs New Afghan Commander," Tuesday, May 03, 2005, "the military has shifted its focus from the fruitless search for fugitives such as Osama bin Laden and Taliban leader Mullah Omar."

When pressed by the *Newsweek* reporters Michael Isikoff and Mark Hosenball to explain how and why the estimate had been revised upward, the president would not give any specifics or backup data. When they asked what methodology had been used to revise their statistic, the White House said the methodology was "classified."

The president's remarks were widely seen and heard, a result of the high impact of his television presence. Any notice that this was bombast, with no hard facts, was invisible.

If there is any realistic evaluation inside the government of the progress being made in the War on Terror, with names and numbers, it is hidden inside the black box of national security. If anyone cries out that the terrorists have not been found and are still at large, their voices are like sounds that you hear in the fog, muffled and indistinct and some immeasurable distance away.

The War on Terror is not about finding terrorists or combating terror. It's about something else.

Chapter Three

THE ETHICAL HEIGHTS
DISAPPEAR IN THE MIST

I HIGHLY RECOMMEND the second season of the TV series *24*. It's *The Perils of Pauline* on crack. Like crack itself, it is neither coherent nor deep, but it is addictive.

Terrorists are about to set off a nuke in Los Angeles. The show is called *24* because it takes place over a twenty-four-hour period. It is urgent! Not only are the terrorists going to nuke L.A., the bomb is going to go off within twenty-four hours.

The most decent, ethical, thoughtful person on the whole show is the American president. You can tell, because he's black. Imagine a dark Colin Powell living in a thriller version of *The West Wing*. He discovers a suspect. Inside his own cabinet! The suspect will not talk. What to do? There are 10 million people in L.A., some of them really hot movie stars and some of them really appealing little tykes and, oh, all sorts of people.

The president not only makes the agonized decision to

torture the suspect, he cranks the dial on the pain machine with his own hand.

This is the essential paradigm in which we live once we have accepted the necessary lie—that the terrorists could not have been stopped by normal means—and have accepted the big lie—that we are in a War on Terror.

These lies make all things acceptable.

Clearly these lies have led to torture at Abu Ghraib and Guantanamo and throughout the entire system. It is clearly the vision that led White House attorneys, including Alberto Gonzales, now our attorney general, and Jay S. Bybee, now a federal appeals court judge, to come up with legal theories that would permit torture. "What if that terrorist knows about the next 9/11, and today is the tenth of September? What then?! It would be irresponsible not to get the information by any means necessary!"

The Second World War was the defining moment of the twentieth century in terms of power and politics.

The Nuremberg Trials were the defining ethical moment. They resulted in the framing of a set of principles that have governed the post—World War II debate on the ethics of war.

THE NUREMBERG PRINCIPLES

Principle I. Any person who commits an act which constitutes a crime under international law is responsible therefor and liable to punishment.

Principle II. The fact that internal law does not impose a penalty for an act which constitutes a crime under international law does not relieve the person who committed the act from responsibility under international law.

Principle III. The fact that a person who committed an act which constitutes a crime under international law acted as Head of State or responsible Government official does not relieve him from responsibility under international law.

Principle IV. The fact that a person acted pursuant to order of his Government or of a superior does not relieve him from responsibility under international law, provided a moral choice was in fact possible to him.

Principle V. Any person charged with a crime under international law has the right to a fair trial on the facts and law.

Principle VI. The crimes hereinafter set out are punishable as crimes under international law:

A. CRIMES AGAINST PEACE

1. Planning, preparation, initiation or waging of a war of aggression or a war in violation of international treaties, agreements or assurances.
2. Participation in a common plan or conspiracy for the accomplishment of any of the acts mentioned under (1).

B. War Crimes

Violations of the laws or customs of war which include, but are not limited to, murder, ill-treatment or deportation of slave-labour or for any other purpose of the civilian population of or in occupied territory, murder or ill-treatment of prisoners of war or persons on the seas, killing of hostages, plunder of public or private property, wanton destruction of cities, towns, or villages, or devastation not justified by military necessity.

C. Crimes Against Humanity

Murder, extermination, enslavement, deportation and other inhumane acts done against any civilian population, or persecutions on political, racial, or religious grounds, when such acts are done or such persecutions are carried on in execution of or in connection with any crime against peace or any war crime.

Principle VII. Complicity in the commission of a crime against peace, a war crime, or a crime against humanity as set forth in Principle VI is a crime under international law.

The idea of war crimes per se was not new. But the idea that there were crimes against humanity was new. Even if it were legal in a given country to murder Jews and Gypsies and homosexuals, it was now a crime against humanity and a crime in international law.

This was radical and revolutionary.

It meant that everyone was responsible for his or her own actions.

If the head of state, or his ministers or generals, decided to exterminate some minority group, or to murder the inhabitants of an entire town as revenge and reprisal for one person's assault on an army officer, or to order medical experiments to see how quickly they could freeze someone to death, or to torture prisoners of war and treat them as subhumans, those were crimes for which they could be tried and punished.

The essence of being in the army or in any truly hierarchical organization is following orders. Here was codified, for the first time, that if a person was ordered to commit a crime—murder, rape, genocide, torture, robbery—it became his right and his duty to say no.

"I was only following orders" was no longer a defense for committing criminal actions.

Despite these clear-cut guidelines, the notion that if we could just torture somebody we could get valuable information and thereby save even one American life, not to mention the thousands who died at the World Trade Center, is seductive.

Consider the temptation to commit torture in the Second World War.

In that war the United States had over a million casualties: 290,000 combat deaths, about 100,000 other deaths, and 670,000 wounded.

When we captured German or Japanese soldiers in World War II, we could be absolutely certain that every single one of them was part of an organization that was dedicated to killing Americans. Those organizations were going to try to do that in the next twenty-four hours, if not in a matter of minutes. Those organizations possessed weapons and of small, medium, and mass destruction.

Our foes had targeted civilian populations, they had used terror as a weapon, they had violated the Geneva Conventions, abused, tortured, and killed prisoners of all nationalities, including Americans.

Despite this catalogue of crimes committed by our enemies, the U.S. military chose to reject torture. One reason for this decision is that we chose to make decent treatment for everyone, even our enemies, one of the ideals for which we were fighting. This policy was clarified in the U.S. Army Field Manual FM 34-52, *Intelligence Interrogation*:[9]

> Revelation of use of torture by U.S. personnel will bring discredit upon the U.S. and its armed forces while undermining domestic and international support for the war effort. It also may place U.S. and allied personnel in enemy hands at greater risk of abuse by their captors. Conversely, knowing the enemy has abused U.S. and allied [prisoners of war] does not justify using methods of interrogation specifically prohibited by [international law] and U.S. policy.

Unlike the prisoners we were taking in World War II, the people we are arresting in Iraq, Afghanistan, and in the United States are not even likely to be our enemies.

According to the *Wall Street Journal* (May 7, 2004), a Red Cross report stated, "Between 70 percent and 90 percent of

9. *Intelligence Interrogation* is available online at www.globalsecurity.org/intell/library/policy/army/fm/fm34-52.

the persons deprived of their liberty in Iraq had been arrested by mistake."

According to a verbal report from a CIA analyst quoted by Seymour Hersh in *Chain of Command: The Road from 9/11 to Abu Ghraib*, at least half the people in Guantanomo don't belong there.

Based on the ratio of arrests to convictions, 96 percent to 98 percent of the people picked up on terrorism-related charges in the United States have a high probability of being innocent.

At a best guess, there were approximately 6,400 federal arrests for terrorism in the United States in the first two years after 9/11. We don't know the numbers after that. The Justice Department stopped releasing figures. With a failure rate in the upper half of the nineties, it's easy to understand why.

The Justice Department claimed that there had been 350 to 400 convictions for terrorist or terrorist-related acts. The Government Accounting Office examined the statistics and found them to be exaggerated by at least 45 percent. For example, they included sixty-five men in New Jersey who attempted to cheat on an English language exam.

As a point of comparison, in New York County, 66 percent of felony arrests lead to a conviction, mostly by plea bargain. If the charges are brought in felony court, which is where all the *Law and Order* cases go, the real-life conviction rate is 92 percent.

The severity of the sentences is another sign of how good the arrests are and how important the crimes are. The Harper's Index collects statistics to wonder at. This pair is from April 2005:

- Number of U.S. residents convicted of "international terrorism" between fall 2001 and fall 2003: 184
- Median sentence given, in days: 14

The other reason that the U.S. military rejected torture and even mistreatment that fell far short of torture is that it doesn't work.

> Experience indicates that the use of prohibited techniques is not necessary to gain the cooperation of interrogation sources. Use of torture and other illegal methods is a poor technique that yields unreliable results, may damage subsequent collection efforts, and can induce the source to say what he thinks the interrogator wants to hear.

> Army Field Manual 34-52,
> *Intelligence Interrogation*

Note the first two words, "experience indicates." Given our basic human reflex to believe that we can beat the truth out of anyone, lots of prisoners, hundreds, possibly thousands, were beaten and burned and tormented in a variety of ways before the military was willing to consider, let alone codify, that the "use of torture and other illegal methods is a poor technique that yields unreliable results."

Torture is forbidden by military law, by treaty, by our own War Crimes Act, and by the Constitution of the United States Code, sections 2340 and 2340A.

The Geneva Convention Against Torture, which

entered into force on June 26, 1987, and became United States law as sections 2340 and 2340A of the United States Code, states:

> No exceptional circumstances whatsoever, whether a state of war or a threat of war, internal political instability or any other public emergency, may be invoked as a justification of torture.

That's about as straightforward and to the point as it can get.

So the White House legal crew of Alberto Gonzales, Jay Bybee, and John Yoo had to really stretch to come up with legal theories that would permit torture.

What they did was create two new classes of people: those who are beneath the law; and those who are above the law.

Initially the only people in the first group, beneath the law, were Al Qaeda members.

Members of the Taliban—that is, anyone fighting U.S. forces in Afghanistan—were quickly added. The theory was that the Geneva Conventions applied only to wars between nations and that Afghanistan was a "failed state," so it didn't count, and people who were captured were not prisoners of war and did not have the rights and status of prisoners of war. This paraphrase may not be fair to the elegance and subtlety of the argument, but that's what they said.

The Geneva Conventions have a section on the treatment and status of civilians in an occupied country. But since the Geneva Conventions were deemed not to apply to Afghanistan, prisoners who were not prisoners of war didn't have the status of civilians either.

They were nothing. They were a new thing.

They were "enemy combatants," sometimes called "unlawful combatants." This was a special class of people with no rights. They couldn't even argue about whether they were properly designated. No lawyers. No letters home. No hearings. No tribunals or judges or juries. Just guards and interrogators.

Then the administration discovered that they could turn American citizens into people beneath the law, too. All they had to do was call a guy an "unlawful combatant"—just give him that label—no procedure, no hearing, no damn judges, no proof—just point a finger and say the words, and as if by magic, he was no longer . . . anything . . . he could no longer call his lawyer or wife or his children to say, "Good-bye, I'm Guantanamo bound." Where he could be beaten. Deprived of sleep. Forced to stand in one position for days. He could be tormented with noise. Force to sleep in his own urine and shit. And interrogated around the clock.

Remember, the point of setting aside the Geneva Conventions was to be able to do that to people. It was to torture people. In the name of finding out on some other September 10 that the planes would fly on September 11. Since many of these unlawful combatants have been in prison since 2001, it is hard to imagine what they might know about what is planned for the day after you read this.

Gonzales, Bybee, and Yoo apparently understood that these actions were war crimes. Like good lawyers, they worried for their clients about what might happen in the future. What if someday, somebody who was not a neoconservative Republican loyalist stumbled into a position of authority at the Justice Department and begin to prosecute people under section 18 of the United States Code 2441, the War Crimes Act.

To deal with that eventuality, they came up with this

theory: the president, when he puts on his commander-in-chief outfit, is above the law. All law. Any law. Including the Constitution. Provided he is acting as a "war leader."

Bybee's memorandum on 2340A, the federal law against torture, says:

> Even if an interrogation method arguably were to violate Section 2340A, the statute would be unconstitutional if it impermissibly encroached on the President's constitutional power to conduct a military campaign.
>
> Any effort to apply Section 2340A in a manner that interferes with the President's direction of such core war matters as the detention and interrogation of enemy combatants thus would be unconstitutional.

They didn't expect George Bush to personally turn up the juice on the alligator clips attached to the tender parts of a "unlawful combatant" like the president in 24, the TV show, did. They expected various minions to do it. The minions needed to be protected against charges that they were committing both common crimes and war crimes. They would be protected because they were acting on the orders of the president, whose powers as commander-in-chief are unlimited.

So here we are at the beginning of the twenty-first century.

White House counsel is recommending that a valid defense against a charge of committing war crimes is, "I was only following orders."

Chapter Four

THERE ARE NO WAR CRIMES
WHEN THE LEGIONS MARCH

———————

THE BUSH ADMINISTRATION wanted to have a war with Iraq. They wanted it before 9/11.

They wanted it even before they came into office.

Bizarre as it may seem, war is illegal.

The Kellogg-Briand Pact of 1928 outlawed aggressive war. Because the participants in the Second World War had signed the treaty, it became the legal foundation for the prosecutions at Nuremberg. There, the underlying principle was reiterated:

> War is essentially an evil thing. Its consequences are not confined to the belligerent states alone, but affect the whole world. To initiate a war of aggression, therefore, is not only an international crime; it is the supreme international crime differing only from other war crimes in that it contains within itself the accumulated evil of the whole.

The Nuremberg Judgment

The Kellogg-Briand Pact remains in force today. According to the textbook used at the International and Operational Law Department at the Judge Advocate General's School of the U.S. Army, "Virtually all commentators agree that the provisions of the treaty banning aggressive war have ripened into customary international law."

The United Nations Charter also outlaws aggressive war. The United States, as a founding member, signed the charter in 1945. It is effectively a treaty, and by signing it we took on treaty obligations.

In addition to trying to keep the peace, the UN Charter permits the United Nations to take collective action. The Korean War and Gulf War One were both UN-sanctioned wars. The Bush administration sought UN approval of their war. It did not receive it.

The lack of a UN mandate does not mean that a nation can't defend itself.

It doesn't even mean that a nation has to be in the midst of an attack before it fights back. It can have a preventive or preemptive war.

That's what the Bush administration decided to have.

When preventive war is argued, the first case usually cited is that of the *Caroline*.

In 1837 there was a rebellion in Canada in the area around Toronto. It was led by William Lyon Mackenzie, "a wiry and peppery little Scotchman." He was "a born agitator," who lost no opportunity to use "his vituperative pen."[10]

"Up then, brave Canadians! Get ready your rifles and

10. www.buffalonian.com/history/articles/1801-50/canrebellion.html.

make short work of it," he cried. And wrote. He had support from Americans in western New York. Mackenzie made one of the Amercians, Rensselaer Van Rensselaer, into a general. They had between twenty-five and two hundred men. They seized Navy Island, which is just above Niagara Falls. Supporters chartered a small steam boat, the *Caroline*, and began to send the rebels (terrorists?) WIDs (weapons of individual destruction) and other supplies. They made several trips.

The *Caroline* returned to Schlosser's Dock, now the town of Niagara Falls, on the American side and put up for the night. The British crossed over in the dark, seized the *Caroline*, killing one American in the process, set her on fire, cut her loose, and let her drift downstream; she went over the Falls in flames.

This event was a cause celebré on both sides of the border and came close to setting off the third Anglo-American war.

The basic concept is one of self-defense.

According to our secretary of state at the time, Daniel Webster, a military action would be legitimate only if "the necessity of that self-defense is instant, overwhelming, and leaving no choice of means and moment for deliberation."

That is, if you could go to the bargaining table and say "Stop!" and ask for an apology and perhaps some reparations and in the meantime no further harm would occur, you were supposed to go to the bargaining table, not launch a military strike. But if, while you were chatting, the *Caroline* would be steaming across the Niagara River with more WIDs and even WmDs (Weapons of medium Destruction), and they would be used to kill your soldiers and citizens, you could preemptively sink her.

Whatever action was taken, it would have to be "nothing unreasonable or excessive; since the act, justified by the necessity of self-defense, must be limited by that necessity, and kept clearly within it."

Blockading the *Caroline* or arresting her captain and crew for smuggling and confiscating the boat and its cargo and forcing the owners to go to court to attempt to reclaim her—had such measures been possible—would have been more clearly within the limits of necessity and more clearly legal than destroying her. Burning and sinking her and killing one man in the process was certainly at the very edge of the envelope. Laying waste the towns of Buffalo and Rochester, even though many of Mackenzie's backers lived there, would have far exceeded the standard of "necessity."

It's a very commonsense sort of standard. The same as the town court judge would use to figure out a bar fight.

It was very hard to argue the necessity for preemptive self-defense in the case of Iraq. Even if Saddam Hussein had wanted to, there was no possible way that Iraq could attack the United States in any conventional manner or with any hope of success. Nor had he done anything that indicated hostile intentions.

It was necessary to make three combined claims:

1. That Saddam had weapons of such force and ferocity that the use of a single one would cause great harm.
2. That Saddam could somehow deliver them against the United States.

    Since he could not invade, it had to be a terrorist scenario. Iraq had supported terrorists in Palestine against Israel. His armies had invaded Iran and Kuwait. But he had never acted against the United States.

The one exception was the accusation that in April 1993, Iraqi intelligence had attempted to assassinate George H. W. Bush with a car bomb while he was making a ceremonial visit to Kuwait. Seymour Hersh, in the *New Yorker*, ("A Case Not Closed," November 1, 1993) cast a great deal of doubt on that story.

So Saddam had to be *linked* to terrorists that were a threat to the U.S., preferably Al Qaeda. They would be his delivery system or he would be their WMD supplier. Either way, it would have the same deadly result.

3. That Saddam had cause or reason or the disposition to attack the United States.

Moreover, all three claims had to have a certain urgency to them. The first question any skeptic asked was: Why now?

On the positive side, if you could argue all three together, there was a kind of overlap, a fog of rhetoric. Simply by putting Saddam in the same sentence as Osama . . .

We know that Iraq and the Al Qaeda terrrorist network share a common enemy—the United States of America.

George W. Bush, Cincinnati, Ohio, October 7, 2002

. . . and weapons of mass destruction in the same sentence with 9/11 . . .

the horror of September 11. We have seen that those who hate America are willing to crash airplanes into buildings full of innocent peple. Our enemies would be no less willing—in fact they would be eager—to use a biological, or chemical, or a nuclear weapon.

George W. Bush, Cincinnati, Ohio, October 7, 2002

. . . it would seem as if they were connected by something more than syntax.

On the negative side, all three claims were false.

Not only were they false, they were obviously false.

THE BIG LIE

The power of the big lie is baffling.

People who see the lie as a lie are puzzled three times over. They can't believe that anyone believes the lie, they can't believe the liar ever thought he would get away with it, and they can't believe that he does get away with it.

there is always a certain force of credibility in the big lie; because the average people of a nation are always more easily manipulated in . . . their emotional nature than consciously or voluntarily; . . . they more readily fall victims to the big lie than the small lie, since they themselves often tell small lies in little matters but would be ashamed to resort to really big lies.

This is not to compare George Bush to Adolf Hitler, who wrote the above in *Mein Kampf*, or Karl Rove to Joseph Goebbels. It is meant merely as an insight from one of the masters of the form on exactly why it was easy to believe that Bill Clinton lied about having sex with that woman and hard to believe that Bush and his entire cabinet were telling bald faced lies about Saddam's connection to Al Qaeda and his weapons of mass destruction.

> It would never come into [average people's] heads to fabricate colossal untruths, and they would not believe that others could have the impudence to distort the truth so infamously.[11]

> *Mein Kampf*

How hard was it to see that there was something wrong with the picture?

Consider: Saddam Hussein was head of a state. He seemed to like that job quite a lot. He had palaces and guards with fancy uniforms, he gave his sons power, he had Western videos and gold-plated toilet bowl handles. He had nothing to gain and everything to lose by making the United States even angrier at him. George Bush knew where to find him, and his country was sitting still to be taken away.

Osama bin Laden lived in a cave. If he had to give up one cave and move to another, so what? His "country" was a set of loose connections, here and there and everywhere. He had a lot to gain from an attack on the U.S.: prestige, status, recruits, and contributions. Classic guerrilla war theory is to provoke The Power in the hopes that the counterstroke will elevate the conflict. Which it did. The United States entered into a series of wars against Arab countries and transformed Osama's nasty little guerrilla

11. Trans. Juergen Buerger (Koln, 2005).

enterprise into an international divide between Islam and the West.

Saddam was our secular bulwark against Islam. He had repressed religion in his own country and gone to war against the Islamic Republic of Iran. Osama was a warrior of Islam. It would have required a miracle for them to have worked together. David Hume established the methodology for judging miracles back in 1748:

> no testimony is sufficient to establish a miracle, unless . . . its falsehood would be more miraculous than the fact which it endeavors to establish.

An Enquiry Concerning Human Understanding

Perhaps miracle is too strong a word. Strange things happen in politics. Stalin and Hitler were allies. Briefly. But extraordinary claims should require extraordinarily strong proof.

To leap over the contradictions, the Bush administration argued that Saddam was a mad dog and cited his invasions of Iran and Kuwait and his use of poison gas against the Iranians and on Kurdish rebels as if he had neither sense nor restraint.

That was, on the face of it, untrue.

Saddam attacked Iran when Iran was in chaos and it seemed to him and everyone else that he would succeed. He also had reason to expect backing from the West. When the Iranians finally stopped him with human-wave counterattacks in which their people were slaughtered by the tens of thousands and began to turn the war around, the United States gave Saddam clandestine help. The U.S. military supplied him with the satellite intelligence that he used to target Iranian troops in order to gas them.

Although the United States publicly condemned the use of gas, Ronald Reagan's special envoy, Donald Rumsfeld, shook Saddam's hand afterward.

U.S. companies had sold Iraq some of the components that went into their biological and chemical weapons, including strains of anthrax and bubonic plague.

This led to the only good joke of the Second Iraq War:

Q: How do we know Iraq has weapons of mass destruction?
A: We kept the receipts.

Before Saddam Hussein invaded Kuwait, he went to the American ambassador, April Glaspie, and asked if it was okay with the United States.

Ambassador Glaspie could have said, "We will defend the sovereignty of any nation," or "We will defend the stability of the Gulf region," or "It would be an aggressive war and therefore a war crime," or she could have told Saddam he should bring his grievances to the United Nations. She said none of those things. Instead she said, "We have no opinion on your Arab-Arab conflicts."

This was not a personal slip on her part. It was America's position. John Kelly, the assistant secretary of state for Near Eastern and South Asian Affairs, in testimony in front of the House Subcommittee on Europe and the Middle East, had this exchange with Congressman Lee Hamilton:[12]

12. Later Hamilton was the vice chairman of the 9/11 Commission.

HAMILTON: If Iraq, for example, charged across the border into Kuwait, for whatever reasons, what would be our position with regard to the use of U.S. forces?

KELLY: That, Mr. Chairman, is a hypothetical or a contingency, the kind of which I can't go into. Suffice it to say we would be extremely concerned, but I cannot get into the realm of "what if" answers.

HAMILTON: In that circumstance, it is correct to say, however, that we do not have a treaty commitment which would obligate us to engage U.S. forces?

KELLY: That is correct.

Here I want to speak from personal experience. I watched the run-up to war. I read the *New York Times* at the coffee shop every morning. I listened to NPR on the radio.

The *New York Times*, both in the news and on the editorial page, claimed that Saddam Hussein had weapons of mass destruction. Judith Miller deserves the Bush Medal of Mass Deception. I have no idea who hypnotized the *Times* editorial board. They have recently woken up, like a group Rip Van Winkle, and are outraged at what has come to pass during their self-imposed sleep.

Nonetheless, I was convinced that Saddam Hussein didn't have weapons of mass destruction and that it didn't matter if he did or didn't, if he cooperated or didn't, we were going to war.

The man who had actually been there, the chief UN weapons inspector from 1991 to 1998, Scott Ritter, said

loudly and clearly that Saddam didn't have any WMD,
declaring in the pages of the *Boston Globe* (July 20, 2002):

> While we were never able to provide 100 percent cer-
> tainty regarding the disposition of Iraq's proscribed
> weaponry, we did ascertain a 90-95 percent level of ver-
> ified disarmament. This figure takes into account the
> destruction or dismantling of every major factory asso-
> ciated with prohibited weapons manufacture, all signif-
> icant items of production equipment, and the majority
> of the weapons and agent produced by Iraq.

In February 2001, Colin Powell had met with the Egyptian
foreign minister, Amre Moussa, and told him the sanctions
"have worked. He has not developed any significant capability with respect to weapons of mass destruction. He is
unable to project conventional power against his neighbors."
This was posted on the U.S. State Department Web site.[13]

On September 12, 2002, George Bush addressed the UN.

13. I now know, but did not know then, that on May 15, 2001, Powell testi-
fied before the Foreign Operations, Export Financing and Related Programs Subcommittee of the Senate Appropriations Committee, and stated:

> The sanctions, as they are called, have succeeded over the last ten
> years, not in deterring him from moving in that direction, but from
> actually being able to move in that direction. The Iraqi regime mili-
> tarily remains fairly weak. It doesn't have the capacity it had ten or
> twelve years ago. It has been contained. And even though we have no
> doubt in our mind that the Iraqi regime is pursuing programs to
> develop weapons of mass destruction—chemical, biological and
> nuclear—I think the best intelligence estimates suggest that they
> have not been terribly successful.

On July 29, 2001, Condoleezza Rice, appearing on *CNN Late Edition with
Wolf Blitzer,* said, "We are able to keep arms from him [Saddam]. His military forces have not been rebuilt."

He said that if they didn't do something about "the grave and gathering danger of Iraq," the U.S. would do it for them. His speech included an onerous set of demands on Iraq. After extensive talks the Security Council passed Resolution 1441 on November 8, 2002, which demanded that Saddam Hussein let the weapons inspectors back in,[14] with full access to places, palaces, and personnel.

To everyone's surprise, Saddam agreed. Truculently, but quickly.

When the inspectors went to Iraq, they got access everywhere they wanted to go. We know this because they told us so. They found nothing.

That was a big problem.

Actually, they did find a few odd warheads and some missiles that could go farther than was permitted. But to put in perspective how well military organizations keep track of their gear, at about the same time there was a report that the U.S. Army had "lost track of 56 airplanes, 32 tanks and 36 Javelin missile command units" (*San Francisco Chronicle*, May 18, 2003), and Donald Rumsfeld at the Department of Defense had said in response to these reports, "According to some estimates we cannot track $2.3 trillion in transactions."

In face of the lack of WMD in Iraq, Colin Powell announced that it didn't matter if the inspectors didn't find anything—it was up to Saddam to prove that he had destroyed everything he was supposed to have destroyed.

The Iraqis tried. They handed in a 12,000-page docu-

14. There is a myth that he threw them out. They were withdrawn in 1998, so that they would be safe when Clinton bombed Iraq. Hussein refused to let them back in. He complained that they had acted as spies for the United States. Which they had.

ment that tracked the destruction of the banned weapons. Before it could even be translated, the United States pronounced it inadequate and proof that Saddam was not in compliance with UN Resolution 1441 and therefore we were going to go to war.

That is, the trigger for the invasion of Iraq was that Saddam Hussein had not kept his receipts.

Actually, failure to comply with 1441, if indeed Saddam had failed to comply, was not supposed to trigger the invasion. The Security Council had spent weeks arguing over two diplomatic-speak phrases: "all necessary means," which would have meant a threat of war, which they rejected, or the one they used, "face serious consequences," which meant go back to the Security Council and figure it out.

The Bush Administration took the position that the UN should have made an invasion the consequence of a failure to comply, and therefore for the UN's own good, the United States was going to invade Iraq.

It all seemed obviously untrue on the face of it. We didn't need the Pentagon Papers or a special commission report or even an exposé by Seymour Hersh to see it.[15]

15. On May 1, 2005, as the final draft of this book was floating back and forth between myself and my editors, the *Times* (of London), published an article headlined "The Secret Downing Street Memo, Secret and Strictly Personal—UK Eyes Only."

The memo was a summary of a meeting of the top people in the British government that took place on July 23, 2002, over going to war with Iraq.

In James Bond movies the head of the secret service is called "M." In real life he is called "C."

C had just been to America and met with George Tenet, head of the CIA, and other officials. This was three months before Bush asked Congress for authorization to go to war and eight months before the invasion. The memo says:

Yet the lies, the intertwined collection of lies, were everywhere and inescapable.

It was as if we had entered a time of mass delusion.

It was the administration that hammered home the lies. With a persistence and commitment that makes it almost impossible to believe that they didn't believe their lies themselves.

They were not alone:

> In the four years since the inspectors left, intelligence reports show that Saddam Hussein has worked to rebuild his chemical and biological weapons stock, his missile delivery capability, and his nuclear program. He has also

C reported on his recent talks in Washington. There was a perceptible shift in attitude. Military action was now seen as inevitable. Bush wanted to remove Saddam, through military action, *justified by the conjunction of terrorism and WMD*. But *the intelligence and facts were being fixed around the policy*. The NSC had no patience with the UN route, and no enthusiasm for publishing material on the Iraqi regime's record. There was little discussion in Washington of the aftermath after military action.

The memo went to say:

The Foreign Secretary said he would discuss this with Colin Powell this week. It seemed clear that Bush had made up his mind to take military action, even if the timing was not yet decided. But *the case was thin. Saddam was not threatening his neighbors, and his WMD capability was less than that of Libya, North Korea or Iran.* (Italics added)

This certainly put it on the record and made it clear enough that Bush and Blair invaded Iraq because they wanted to and that they knew that "the case was thin" and that "the intelligence and facts were being fixed."

In the weeks that followed the publication in the UK, this remained a fog fact in America. Over two weeks it dribbled out on page 16 or 22, got a couple of mentions on CNN, and Molly Ivans gave it a column. But nobody in the mainstream media ran with it like it was Monica Lewinsky performing oral sex.

given aid, comfort, and sanctuary to terrorists, including Al Qaeda members.

Senator Hillary Clinton (D-NY), October 10, 2002

We are in possession of what I think to be compelling evidence that Saddam Hussein has, and has had for a number of years, a developing capacity for the production and storage of weapons of mass destruction.

Senator Bob Graham (D-FL), December 8, 2002

The threat of Saddam Hussein with weapons of mass destruction is real.

Senator John F. Kerry (D-MA), January 23, 2003

There was no opposition. Nobody ever said: Let's find out if he has such weapons. Let us do only that which is necessary for our self-defense, like take them away.

There was only delusion.

The Coalition of the Willing invaded. Saddam's army folded. All those white suits and gas masks turned out to be unnecessary (but better safe than sorry). No weapons of mass destruction were found.

Two postwar teams went looking. The first was led by David Kay, the second by Charles Duelfer. Both wrote reports that said there were no WMDs or active programs.

The Senate Intelligence Committee and the 9/11 Commission both found that there were no connections between Saddam Hussein and 9/11 or Al Qaeda.

Hitler said that the thing about Big Lies is that it doesn't matter if the liars are caught:

Even though the facts which prove the liars are lying are brought out clearly, the people will still doubt they are liars and think there must be some other explanation. The thing about really outrageous lies is that even after they have been completely nailed as falsehoods, they are still out there and believed. All the expert liars in this world and all who conspire together in the art of lying know it.

Mein Kampf

The last of the reports was the Duelfer Report. It appeared in October 2004. Just afterward, but before the election, an organization called the Program on International Policy Attitudes, working with a polling company, Knowledge Networks, did a poll about people's beliefs concerning 9/11 and the Iraq War. They divided the interview subjects into Bush supporters and Kerry supporters and compared how they answered two questions:

BUSH SUPPORTERS

1. DID SADDAM HAVE WMD OR WMD PROGRAMS?

72 percent believed that Saddam had WMDs or major programs to develop them.
56 percent believed that most experts agreed with them that Saddam had WMDs or WMD programs.

57 percent believed that the Duelfer report
said that there were WMDs or WMD
programs in Iraq.

2. WAS SADDAM CONNECTED TO 9/11 OR AL QAEDA?

75 percent believed that Saddam was connected to 9/11 or to Al Qaeda.

56 percent thought the 9/11 Commission
report said Saddam was connected to 9/11
or to Al Qaeda.

Kerry supporters were more accurate.

Yet even 30 percent of the Kerry supporters thought
Iraq was involved with 9/11 or Al Qaeda and 27 percent
thought that the 9/11 Commission report said so. Even after
search after search failed to turn up WMDs or WMD programs in Iraq, 27 percent of Kerry supporters still thought
that WMDs had been found there.

It is literally true to say that Bush was elected by the
delusional.

If the lies did nothing else, they held at bay questions about
the real reasons for the invasion of Iraq.

There is little doubt that the administration wanted to
invade Iraq before Bush was even sworn in.

Secretary of Defense Donald Rumsfeld, Assistant Secre-
tary of Defense Paul Wolfowitz, Assistant Secretary of State
Richard Armitage, Undersecretaries of State John Bolton
and Paula Dobriansky, Presidential Adviser for the Middle
East Elliott Abrams, and Bush's special Iraq envoy, Zalmay
Khalilzad, had all signed a letter in 1998 to Bill Clinton

urging him to go to war in Iraq, without bothering with UN approval, to remove Saddam Hussein.

The 2000 Republican Party platform called for the removal of Saddam Hussein.

Bush's treasury secretary, Paul O'Neill, said, "From the very first instance, it was about Iraq. It was about what we can do to change this regime."

Counterterrorism Adviser Richard Clarke said that after the 9/11 attacks, "George Bush wanted me to come back with a report that said Iraq did this." A story in the *Washington Post* (March 22, 2004) quoted Clarke as saying:

> At first I was incredulous that we were talking about something other than getting Al Qaeda. I realized with almost a sharp physical pain that Rumsfeld and Wolfowitz were going to try to take advantage of this national tragedy to promote their agenda about Iraq. Since the beginning of the administration, indeed well before, they had been pressing for a war with Iraq. My friends in the Pentagon had been telling me that the word was we would be invading Iraq sometime in 2002.

One of the reasons for the invasion was oil.

Another is the vision of a Pax Americana: a world ruled by the United States for the world's own good in which the U.S. makes sure to maintain its preeminence as the sole superpower. To do this, we need "forward bases" in strategic spots around the globe, particularly the oil-rich Middle East.

What ties that together? The thing that made it Iraq,

instead of some other little country, were the political experiences of George Bush and his close circle.

There is a story from Russ Baker. It only has a single source, which is why it ended up on Guerrilla News Network instead of some more "reputable" publication. Baker interviewed Mickey Herskowitz, a professional ghostwriter who had been hired to do Bush's campaign autobiography. Herskowitz told Baker he had met with the candidate about twenty times to talk to him for the book:

> [George Bush] said to me: "One of the keys to being seen as a great leader is to be seen as a commander-in-chief." And he said, "My father had all this political capital built up when he drove the Iraqis out of Kuwait and he wasted it." He said, "If I have a chance to invade . . . if I had that much capital, I'm not going to waste it. I'm going to get everything passed that I want to get passed and I'm going to have a successful presidency."

Imagine being George Bush and watching your father, as president of the United States, soar to unprecedented heights in the polls, then slide and slide and be beaten by that liberal piece of trailer-park trash, Bill Clinton.

That's a life lesson.

Whether or not the Herskowitz story is verifiable almost doesn't matter, for it draws our attention to what the experience must have been like and it fits with our notions both of human nature and of Bush's actual behavior in office.

The circle around Bush today was around his father

then. They would have experienced the same exhilaration and the same crushing disappointment. Though it would have been less personal.

The story also places the Second Iraq War in a historical context. According to Herskowitz, said Baker:

> George W. Bush's beliefs on Iraq were based in part on a notion dating back to the Reagan White House—ascribed in part to now Vice President Dick Cheney, chairman of the House Republican Policy Committee under Reagan. "Start a small war. Pick a country where there is justification you can jump on, go ahead and invade."

> Bush's circle of preelection advisers had a fixation on the political capital that accrued to Britain's Prime Minister Margaret Thatcher from the Falklands War. Said Herskowitz: "They were just absolutely blown away, just enthralled by the scenes of the troops coming back, of the boats, people throwing flowers at [Thatcher] and her getting these standing ovations in Parliament and making these magnificent speeches."

> Republicans, Herskowitz said, felt that Jimmy Carter's political downfall could be attributed largely to his failure to wage a war. He noted that President Reagan and President Bush's father himself had (besides the narrowly focused Gulf War I) successfully waged limited wars against tiny opponents—Grenada and Panama—and gained politically.

While all this was going on, another story was gaining momentum almost completely under the radar.

After the Kellogg-Briand Pact, the Nuremberg Trials, and the creation of the United Nations, the logical next step was the creation of a permanent, international war crimes court.

It was proposed at a UN meeting in Rome in 1998. One hundred twenty-four countries voted in favor, and seven countries voted against it: China, Iraq, Libya, Yemen, Qatar, Israel, and the United States.

American opposition to the court was based on the feeling that because it is the United States that most often goes out on peacekeeping missions and that has the most military personnel around the world, its troops are the most exposed to complex, unpredictable, tense situations. Also, Americans feel, perhaps rightly, that there is a lot of unjustified anti-Americanism out there and the idea of some jacked-up hick from Kyrgyzstan or Rwanda accusing some clean-cut young Marine, who was just there saving the world, of doing something heinous and then having that fine young man or woman be judged by unreliable, untrustworthy, probably uneducated, Third World UN types, who would like nothing better than to slander and defame America's good name, was just too terrible to contemplate.

The International Criminal Court Treaty would go into effect once sixty countries had ratified it. The treaty describes the crimes within the jurisdiction of the court as follows:

> The jurisdiction of the Court shall be limited to the most serious crimes of concern to the international community as a whole. The Court has jurisdiction in accordance with this Statute with respect to the following crimes:

(a) The crime of genocide;
(b) Crimes against humanity;
(c) War crimes;
(d) The crime of aggression.

On December 31, 2000, President Clinton signed the treaty. The court opened in July 2002. But without the United States. On May 6, 2002, President George W. Bush, had unsigned the treaty.

This was unprecedented. No American president had ever unsigned a treaty that a president before him had signed. No nation in the world had ever unsigned a UN treaty that it had signed.

In addition, the United States began demanding bilateral "impunity agreements" from countries that had signed the treaty, whose purpose was to exempt U.S. personnel from being charged in those countries of crimes as defined by the treaty.

The first American century, the twentieth, was marked by egalitarian principles and the belief that we should all be equal under the law, as people and as nations. The chief prosecutor at the Nuremberg Trials for war crimes, U.S. Associate Supreme Court Justice Robert Jackson, said:

> Certain acts in violations of treaties are crimes whether the United States does them or whether Germany does them, and we are not prepared to lay down a rule of criminal conduct against others which we would not be willing to have invoked against us.

The second American century—should it be so—has begun by initiating a three-tier system of international justice.

There are those who are meant to abide by the law. There are those who are beneath the law—failed states and rogue states that can be invaded at will. Then there is the Imperium. That's us. Our legions may not be judged by any but their own. They act with impunity. They are above the law.

Chapter Five

DISBELIEVING WHAT WE'RE SEEING

_____

ON MAY 2, 2003, George Bush spent millions of dollars[16] of our money to make a five-minute movie of himself as a "Top Gun."

U.S. Navy carrier pilots—the equal of professional stunt pilots anywhere—flew a Navy S-3B Viking, with "Commander in Chief" painted on the tail and on the fuselage, out from San Diego and landed it on the carrier USS *Abraham Lincoln.* After they landed it, George Bush, who

16. Congressman Henry Waxman's office suggests $1 million. He represents California's 30th congressional district, which includes old Hollywood, Santa Monica, Malibu, Bel Air, Brentwood, and Topanga. The Bush administration takes the position that the ship was there anyway—well sort of there, nearby, at least, and they only had to move it a short way and maneuver it to get the light right for the cameras and keep the sailors at sea just one more day—and the president was going to fly out anyway and so the only number that should be counted is the difference between a helicopter and an S-3B jet, by the hour, which is not much.

Another way to look at it is the cost of an aircraft carrier, by the day. The projected annual savings of decommissioning a carrier divided by the number of days in the year is $19,178,000.

had been their passenger, stepped out. He wore a pilot's costume, complete with a helmet and the codpiece effect created by the harness straps that framed his crotch.

Just as if they were watching a shot of Tom Cruise walking away from an F-14, the audience understood that they were supposed to assume that Bush had been the pilot. It's innate to the way our minds work. Sergei Eisenstein, one of the founders of modern cinema, labeled it "the montage effect." Given a sequence of images, viewers will create a connection between them. They will invent in their own minds the necessary information to create a coherent narrative. This is the fundamental syntax of the language of film. Eisenstein said it was the way to manipulate emotions.

At the movies it takes an act of will to stay conscious that it is not Tom in the jet. It's not a huge effort, but it needs some alertness. So too, with the staging of reality.

The media did not exercise their will. They entered into the illusion. The theatrical term for that, to the degree that we do it ourselves, is "the willing suspension of disbelief." In this case the media, as a whole, suspended their disbelief and transmitted that credulous condition to us.

COMMANDER IN CHIEF LANDS ON USS *LINCOLN*

ABOARD USS *ABRAHAM LINCOLN* (CNN)— President Bush made a landing aboard the USS *Abraham Lincoln* Thursday . . .[17]

17. The rest of the headline *does* say: "arriving in the co-pilot's seat of a Navy S-3B Viking after making two fly-bys of the carrier." The careful reader may parse that and understand that he was a passenger. But video, the photos, and the headline are likely to leave the parsers behind. CNN is, as these things go, a relatively neutral purveyor of information. And their coverage here was typical, not atypical.

"Yes, I flew it. Yeah, of course, I liked it," Bush said. No doubt at some point in the flight he had taken the controls. That enabled him to make the statement without it being a literal lie. CNN added that he "was an F-102 fighter pilot in the Texas Air National Guard."

When he emerged, he was greeted by cheering throngs of sailors in front of the "Mission Accomplished" banner. The banner became controversial. First because the administration tried to claim that it had been a spontaneous gesture on the part of the sailors when it had not been. It had been ordered and placed by the White House prop department. And later because the mission had clearly not been accomplished. But the event had done what it needed to do. It made the president look like a real fighter pilot. Cheered and beloved by his fellow troops.

He had sent the country into two wars and had famously announced, "I'm a war president," with the swaggering bluster of a cheerleader who finally makes it to the varsity and announces, "Now you can't mess with me."

The warrior image rested, at least in part, on Bush's service to his country as a young man in time of war. He said things like, "I've been to war. I've raised twins. If I had a choice, I'd rather go to war." He portrayed himself as a gung-ho kind of guy who had rushed down to his recruiting station and signed up for the Texas Air National Guard to become a fighter pilot, ready to take to the those dangerous skies to smite the enemy.

If that story line could be shown to be false, then all that rested on it might be thrown into question.

If it could be shown to be a lie, and the lie could be made to stick, and could be turned into a reference point, then all the other instances of manufacturing illusions would begin to fall into a category and automatically acquire labels and they would all emerge from the fog, like zombies from the night in *Dawn of the Dead*.

Would that be a good thing?

Or would all of it be just the kind of vicious, back-stabbing, tear-the-leader-down noise we have come to expect in politics? In the treatment of all celebrities?

Republicans like to say, "Character matters."

- "It is the character of the presidency that matters!"—Rush Limbaugh, Rush Online
- "Yes, character matters!"—Gary Livacari, *The GW Hatchet*
- "Character Matters. . . . Clinton . . . didn't have the integrity to be president."—Jonah Goldberg, editor at large, *National Review* Online
- "Character Matters."—Craig Silver, chairman, International Christian Concern
- "Character matters. More than anything else."—This Week with the Chicowitz (blog)
- "Character matters. . . . President George Bush is a real man. Glad I voted for him."—Something's Rotten (blog)
- "Presidential character matters."—William Bennett, *The Death of Outrage: Bill Clinton and the Assault on American Ideals* (jacket copy)
- "Character does matter."—Lucas Morel, adjunct fellow, Ashbrook Center for Public Affairs, Ashland University
- *A Matter of Character: Inside the White House of George W. Bush*—Ronald Kessler

For Republicans, "character" mostly consists of having a penis placed securely inside the confines of a hetero-sexual marriage. Still, cheerleading for war while ducking out of it yourself does testify to a distinct hypocrisy, and it was the one that permeated the administration. There's a full list of the chickenhawks on the *New Hampshire Gazette* Web site.[18] Besides the president and vice president, some of the highlights are Jeb Bush, Tom DeLay, Newt Gingrich, Richard Perle, Trent Lott, Dick Armey, and Paul Wolfowitz. According to a report in the *Guardian* (August 20, 2002), Rush Limbaugh got out of military service with either "anal cysts" or an "ingrown hair follicle on his bottom."

Hypocrisy is a subject worthy of study. Hypocrisy, like lying, is necessary to the social fabric. People prefer varying degrees and kinds of hypocrisy. Kerry had served in Vietnam and then come back and said the war was bad. Many Republicans were apoplectic in their hatred of him as a result. Kerry may have lost the election because of it or, more specifically, for not understanding how deeply he had offended against hypocrisy.

Bush had not served, at least not at the front, but he supported the war. Most Republicans loved him for this.

Many Democrats thought that Clinton's sexual antics were not a fit subject for political debate because his private life was irrelevant to policy. Is Bush's military record an aspect of his "character" that is actually relevant to policy, or is it just trash-talking?

The empirical evidence that his service record mattered is

18. www.nhgazette.com/cgi-bin/NHGstore.cgi?user_action=list&category=%20NEWS%3B%20Chickenhawks.

that whatever opposition there was inside the administration to the war in Iraq came from Colin Powell and the military. They were also the ones who said: If we are going in, we should go with a larger force. Vietnam had been a lesson in what it can cost to be an occupying power. Actually being in a war might have made Bush slower to start his own war and, if he did start one, might have made him more thorough in the planning and more prepared to finish it.

On the other hand, it may well have been the complete lack of firsthand knowledge that gave Bush the blind, oblivious bravura to charge into Iraq like he was playing a video game that he could win quickly because he had selected an "easiest" level of play. According to Reverend Pat Robertson, Bush said, with great certainty, "We're not going to have any casualties." And he clearly thought it would be over when the tanks rolled into Baghdad, except for throwing roses and pulling down big statues.

The 2004 presidential election could have—and from the Democrats' point of view, should have—turned into a battle between the Combat Evader and the War Hero, between the spoiled rich kid, a phony and a hypocrite, and the real deal, a man who had done his duty and who even had the courage, when he came home, to speak up and say what was wrong with the war in which he had three times shed his own blood.

But it didn't.

Instead it became a contest between the War President, tough and manly, who stayed the course, and the Flip Flopper, who was effete and elite and soft on terror.

How did it happen?

Clearly the Democrats and the Kerry campaign failed to capitalize on the story of how Bush had shirked his duty as a young man. Nor did the media make much of it. We don't really expect the media to run with a story because it is meaningful or to take a story and develop its meaning for us. But there was lots of potential for scandal in this one. There were backroom deals, files were apparently "sanitized," and there was a cover-up. It contained several of the rare instance in which Bush told specific, documentable lies, something he is normal very good at avoiding.

It was only at the very last moment that *Sixty Minutes* tried to make something of it. In their urgency to get there in time and because of the nature of news as it is practiced— as scandal-mongering structured around "fresh evidence" and "smoking guns"—they stumbled. Bush emerged unscathed. *Sixty Minutes*, CBS News, the "liberal media," investigative journalism, and Dan Rather took the hit.

Chapter Six

DON'T LISTEN TO WHAT THEY SAY—LOOK AT WHAT THEY DO

IN JANUARY 2005, in his State of the Union message, George Bush said: "Justice is distorted and our economy is held back by irresponsible class actions and frivolous asbestos claims, and I urge Congress to pass legal reforms this year."

Dick Cheney sat on the dias behind the president and smirked. Was he smirking because he was certain that this was a fog fact and would remain so?

Cheney smirks often. He has a lot to smirk about. Rarely in history has anyone gotten over so often for so much so shamelessly. Bush is also a smirker. But the Bush smirk is quick, like a wink, which sometimes accompanies his smirk. The Cheney smirk is a steadier sneer, a constant inner flame of appreciation of the world's credulity, or perhaps of his own superiority.

Still, this smirk seemed to have a certain particularity about it. After all, the president of the United States is only mandated by the Constitution to give one speech a year. He had just used that speech, his most important forum, to announce that he was putting his full power and prestige behind a bill to rescue a single corporation. That corporation had already received all sorts of gifts, no-bid contracts, and contracts with guaranteed profits for the privatization of the army and then for the "reconstruction" of Iraq. The reason that they still needed rescuing was because of their previous bad management. By the man smirking behind him.

George Bush was demanding a "save Halliburton" law.

He was doing it right in our faces, on prime-time television, on all the networks plus Fox and CNN and PBS and NPR, in front the entire Senate and many congressmen. And no one said a word.

It was only one line, but it was there with the big items: the war in Iraq, threatening Syria and Iran with wars, dismantling Social Security and our current system of taxation.

In the week after the speech, I was not able to find a single story that even hinted at what that one line was really about. Or that discussed any of the history that lay behind it: the president's private business career; Cheney's road to riches; the asbestos industry and asbestos litigation.

All of these should be at least moderately common knowledge. They're all great stories and extremely instructive.

THE TALE OF BUSHENOMICS

The proposal to pass a "save Halliburton" law is the tip of the iceberg that is Bushenomics.

Bushenomics is very simple. It is about taking public tax dollars and giving it to rich people.

The genius of Bush is in selling it to the voters as something that's good for them.

Any appearance of benefits to low and middle-income people is there to sell the programs. Whatever benefits there are will be more than offset by increases in other taxes, the loss of services, and the accumulation of debts that will at some point have to be paid off with interest.

The story that tax cuts for the rich will stimulate the economy so much that they will solve all the problems is also bogus. This was originally, under Reagan, called trickle-down economics, one of those inadvertently great right-wing names that really is a euphemism for piss on the poor. Under Bush Sr., the name was changed to Supply Side Economics; and under this Bush, it's called a stimulus package.

It didn't work then . . .

Remember Ronald Reagan and Supply Side Economics? In the early 1980s, Reagan promised the nation that if we lowered tax rates on the wealthy, the economy would grow so much the federal budget would be balanced "within three years, maybe even two." . . .

The results, we now know, were a disaster. In 1982, the first full year after the tax cuts were enacted, the economy actually shrank 2.2%, the worst performance since the Great Depression. And the effect on the federal budget was catastrophic. . . .

Clinton . . . intentionally reversed the Supply Side Formula, raising taxes on the wealthy and reducing them on the lowest wage earners . . . [and] the U.S. economy produced the longest sustained economic expansion in U.S. history . . . 18 million new jobs, the highest . . . ever. Inflation fell . . . real interest rates fell

. . . greatest housing boom ever . . . economic growth averaged 4% a year compared to 2.8% average growth over the 12 years of Reagan/Bush.

Rarely in public affairs do we have the luxury of such starkly clear, empirically proven, historically sound contrasts.[19]

. . . and it doesn't work now.

Bush's tax cut, his Medicare program, the privatization of Social Security, and the change in the tax codes are all about the transfer of wealth to the wealthy.

In 2004, the nation's 275,000 millionaires reaped over $30 billion from the Bush tax cuts.

The average tax cut for someone making a million dollars a year was $123,592.[20]

The average tax cut for someone in the middle 20 percent of income was $647.

The disproportion will increase over time as the estate-tax cut and other tax cuts come into effect.

Additional plans to change taxes call for the elimination of taxes on the types of income, such as dividends and capital gains, that you can acquire while you sit in the Bahamas and the cabana boy brings you a rum punch with a pink paper umbrella stuck into a pineapple chunk.

The tax burden will be shifted to those working for their money or will be made up by a national sales tax.

Bush's drug benefits for the elderly benefit the pharmaceutical companies far more than they do old people. Especially if

19. Robert Freeman, "Bush's Tax Cuts: A Form of National Insanity," *Counterpunch*, May 30, 2003, www.counterpunch.org/freeman05302003.html.

20. This is the average based on all taxes cut, not just income tax.

the cost of the program bankrupts the system. Which is actually likely to happen.

Bush's plan to privatize Social Security is quite simply and literally a plan to divert money from people to corporations. It's simple and deserves a simple explanation.

Currently, the way Social Security works is as a flow-through system. You pay in money. It is paid out to your parents. When your children go to work, they will put in money that goes to you when you are retired.

A privatized system is a pension system. You put in money. It goes into some sort of investment. If you're lucky, it increases. It might decrease. When you retire, you get your money. Plus or minus.

If we try to switch systems, the money that is flowing in has to be diverted. It will go into stocks and bonds and real estate. It will go through salesmen and brokers who will take a little or a lot off the top.

That means there is no money to flow out. Because it's been diverted to businesses and corporations. Where it has to sit until your retirement.

But there is a commitment by the government to the people that the money is supposed to flow to. To us. It is a contract. And if it's not paid, there will be a whole lot of old people moving in with their children or begging in the streets. So the money that will be diverted now must be replaced.

How can it be replaced? Through taxation or borrowing. If it is borrowed, it will have to be repaid, with interest. Since it is a government debt, taxpayers will have to pay the original debt plus the interest.

This is class warfare. It is the re-creation of the distance between rich and poor.

Fair enough. That's what being a Republican is supposed to be about.

But it's also supposed to be about balancing the budget, which was item number one on Newt Gingrich's Republican Contract with America. Gingrich called for:

> The Fiscal Responsibility Act: A balanced budget/tax limitation amendment and a legislative line-item veto to restore fiscal responsibility to an out-of-control Congress, requiring them to live under the same budget constraints as families and businesses.

And that's where things turn strange and incomprehensible. Inexplicable, perhaps even pathological.

When George Bush came into office, there was a budget surplus. There was a plan in place to keep on accumulating surpluses and pay down the deficit.

This is what is bad about deficits.

If you have ever run up a credit-card debt, you discover that you quickly reach a point where a large part of your monthly payment is just for interest. Sometimes your entire monthly payment must go to paying interest. Then you can't buy any goods and services. And you still owe the principal.

You will also notice, the more you are paying in interest, the harder it is to pay off principle and reduce the size of the interest payments.

If the government has a surplus, it can pay off its debts. If it pays its debts it pays less interest. It can buy more goods and services with the same amount of tax revenue. Just as you can buy more goods and services with the same salary if your credit card is paid up and there are no interest charges.

Back in 1991, when George Bush the First was in office,

about 34 percent of our tax revenues went to interest payments on government debts that had been racked up by Republican administrations.[21] That was the highest percentage ever.

Under Clinton, that amount declined to the 24 percent range and was headed even lower.[22]

But George decided to give the money away.

He said it was "our" money. Not the government's. Therefore it should go back to us.

But the government is us. It is our collective tool to organize protection and stability and a host of other things that seem to work better when done as a society. One of the things we had done with this collective tool was accumulate debts that now needed to be paid. One of the things we could have done with "our" surplus was pay down "our" debts so that less of "our" money would go to interest and "our" government could buy more goods and services with "our" continuing tax contributions.

Bush also said that by giving that money away he would stimulate the economy to the point where it would create so much money that it would pay back more than he had given away.

It did not do so. Nor did it create jobs. Which was the other promise.

---

21. That does not mean that a third of our budget went to interest. The budget was larger than the amount of revenue (we were creating deficits at the time), so a third of the revenue would be some smaller number of the budget.

22. The percentage of the budget paid in interest was 14 percent in 1999, projected to be down to 10 percent in 2002. Under Clinton's plan, all debt that could be eliminated would have been eliminated by 2013.

Clinton argued that lower debt meant lower interest rates for everyone and that it had already fueled economic growth and would continue to do so. It would create room to deal with the Medicare and Social Security problems without turning them into crises.

Between the time Bush came into office and July 2004, 2,600,000 jobs were lost.[23]

So in August 2004 Bush announced a new "economic plan"—that is, a new round of tax cuts. The plan would cost $670 billion dollars, and, he claimed, it would create 2.1 million new jobs over the next three years.[24]

This is where it gets really bizarre. During the eight years of the Clinton administration, 18 million new jobs were created. That's an average of 2.25 million per year, 6.75 million for a three-year period. While a budget surplus was being created. Bush had a plan with a job-creation rate of just one third that of Clinton's, which was predicted to increase the deficit by another $670 billion dollars, and he was bragging about it!

It gets weirder still. None of the major media compared the "bold" economic plan with the available record—Clinton's record.

Here's the pathetic part. While the Democrats did point out that there were better ways to create jobs, they failed to compare Bush's anemic goals to their own robust record.

Having squandered the surplus and having nothing to show for it, Bush went on a kind of rampage, throwing away more and more money with more and more tax cuts—with the deficits running at $400 billion to $500 hundred billion a year, he was pushing to make his tax cuts permanent at a cost estimated to be $2.1 trillion over ten years—while spending more and more money, as if it was his goal to create deficits, big deficits, record deficits, incomprehensibly huge deficits.

23. factcheck.org/article101.html.

24. www.cnn.com/2003/ALLPOLITICS/01/07/economic.stimulus/ "Bush: Urgent Need for 'Bold' Economic Plan," Wednesday, January 8, 2003.

Deficits that will, unchecked, bankrupt the country. Before that happens, foreign investors, who have already taken a hit of as much as 40 percent on their dollar holdings, will likely get out of the dollar, causing it to collapse, and our economy with it.

There are two questions. The first is: Why?

The most rational answer I've come across is that it's a game of chicken to force the Democrats, when they see us driving straight to the destruction of Social Security or the collapse of the republic, to flinch first and recommend a raise in taxes. Then the Republicans can call them "tax-and-spend" Democrats again. They hated that Clinton had robbed them of the use of that epithet.

Another possibility is that bankrupting the country (or at least the government) is intentional. The economist Paul Krugman, in his *New York Times* column of March 4, 2005, wrote, "Mr. Bush celebrated the budget's initial slide into deficit. In the summer of 2001 he called plunging federal revenue 'incredibly positive news' because it would 'put a straitjacket' on federal spending."

Bush's remark four years earlier was little noted when it was made. It's part of what is so peculiar about all of this. It's being done in plain sight yet it is unseen.

Our expectations of sanity and probity make it hard for us to believe that our leaders are recklessly senseless.

As I wrote this passage in early 2005, I knew there were many antigovernment true believers who believe that government should be destroyed and bad economic policies are a way to do this. I also knew that "they" have been trying to do it for a long time. David Stockman, Ronald Reagan's budget director, said the deficits they created back then were intended to bankrupt the government. Other members of the Reagan administration have privately confirmed that they wanted to create a financial crisis that would require the government to be shut down, except for certain basics—the military and interest payments on the debt. They most especially wanted to destroy the regulatory agencies, such as OSHA and the EPA, and to destroy Social Security. Grover Norquist, the president of Americans for Tax Reform, is one of the most visible spokesmen for this point of view. He calls it "starving the beast."

I knew all that, but still, it's like driving a perfectly good Buick sedan off a cliff because you think you should be driving a Porsche Cayenne and, God damn it, that'll make the insurance company pay for it! Most people, even if they have those thoughts, once they get the keys to the car and get out on Mulholland Drive and head for the edge, they stop. Because people don't drive cars over cliffs.

But on February 4th, Bush announced the 2005 budget.

It sets the self-destruction of the government explicitly in motion. It's not exactly driving it over the cliff. It's putting the car on a slope nearby and letting it roll backward over the edge.

It works like this. The budget sets overall spending caps for discretionary items for the next five years. Those caps are to be mandatory. At the same time, it asks for certain levels of expenditures for the military, homeland security, and certain international programs. If those requests are met, it will bring the spending very close to the caps.

To meet the caps, it will be necessary to cut in other areas. The administration is careful not to say where. But the things that are left are education, environmental protection, veterans' health care, medical research, law enforcement, and food and drug safety inspection.

This is devious and destructive. Like playing chicken or driving cars over cliffs, if you do them when you're over twenty-one and you're supposed to be a responsible adult who knows the consequences, they are pathological.

Justin A. Frank, M.D., the psychiatrist who wrote *Bush on the Couch*, is perfectly willing to say that our president is exactly that.[25] He believes that Bush's deepest wish is to destroy, that Bush is a sadist who takes particular delight in hurting those who need help and compassion, and that this budget process is ultimately designed to do that.

We should be very familiar with the pattern of Bush's pathology from watching serial killer movies and forensic psychologists on TV.

Each act becomes more blatant, brazen, and flagrant.

First there was the demolition of the surplus. Bush announced a tax cut and said he was giving us our own money back and that that was the best thing to do with it. It was possible to believe that he was sincere.

Then came the second round of tax cuts, which he called a jobs-and-stimulus package. That sounded sensible. Downright Keynesian.[26] Even liberal. Didn't JFK do something like that?

After 9/11, there was big spending. Homeland Security.

25. Frank, *Bush on the Couch: Inside the Mind of the President* (New York: HarperCollins, 2004).

26. John Maynard Keynes was a British economist who invented the idea of deficit spending to stimulate the economy, especially at times of high unemployment. The method he recommended was investment in public works, which would employ people—immediately solving the unemployment issue—who would then have money to spend, and the aggregate total of spending and consumption would increase, boosting the entire economy.

That's demand-side economics.

Supply-side economics is the Republican inversion of the idea. It is that

And wars. We needed that. Had to do that. At that point, we might have reversed course on the tax cuts. But who would say so? "Tax cuts, tax cuts, we'll give you tax cuts" had been the cry of the Republicans for so many years, how could they now say: That's irresponsible. And how could the Democrats, beaten with the stick of "The Democrats will raise your taxes," stand up and say: Let's take the tax cuts back! So Bush became a cut-and-spend Republican with hardly a word of alarm.

Then there was the Medicare bill. Even with all the cuts in revenue and the rise in spending, Bush and the Republican Congress jammed through this piece of legislation. It was sold to Congress and the American people as costing $400 billion over ten years. Richard S. Foster, chief actuary for the Medicare program, testified that he was forced, on threat of being fired, not to tell Congress that his numbers said that the program would really cost $534 billion. On February 9, 2005, the *Washington Post* reported that even that figure had to be revised upward: "Medicare chief Mark B. McClellan . . . acknowledged that the cumulative cost of the program between 2006 and 2015 will reach $1.2 trillion, but he cited several major savings and offsets that he said will reduce the federal government's bottom-line cost to $720 billion."

By 2004, the proof was on the table. Bush's tax cuts had produced a growing deficit and the worst job-creation record since Herbert Hoover.

It must be said that if Bush believes what he says—that his tax cuts have helped—he is not alone. This is important

---

you give the money to the investing class and they will supply more things which the unemployed will want so much that they will . . . they will . . . rob convenience stores to obtain them.

in a diagnosis. The number of people who believe in something, irrespective of how illogical it is, is one of the primary
factors that separates a clinically delusional belief from a
common religious belief.

The FactCheck article cited above for the job numbers
goes on to say; "Economists are virtually unanimous in
saying that the tax cuts that have taken place have created
jobs. . . . Implying that tax cuts are not contributing to job
growth deserves an "F" in freshman economics."

Gosh, that put me in my place. Reading that, it's hard for
me to even remember that except for two months, Bush's
job creation lagged behind population growth and he ended
his first term with only 114,000 jobs added. As compared to
Clinton's 9 million. As the guys at FactCheck.org like to say,
"Who are you gonna believe? Me or your lying eyes?"

The best estimates were that it would cost $4.2 trillion to
make the tax cuts permanent. With fervor, with conviction,
with a smirk and a wink, he campaigned to do just that.

Then he moved to privatize Social Security.

The world seemed very surprised by that, although he
had announced it several times, most prominently in his
acceptance speech at the Republican National Convention,
where he said, "Many of our most fundamental systems—the
tax code, health coverage, pension plans, worker training,
were created for a world of yesterday, not tomorrow. We will
transform these systems."

This was fairly explicit. Yet sufficiently vague that
nobody, not our leading newspapers, not CNN, not CBS, not
NPR or PBS, not even the Internet lefties, jumped up and
down and freaked out and said, "He wants to do what?!"

He did not at that time outline exactly how he meant to
"transform" those systems. But he used the word "trans-

form," not "modify," "tune up," "rescue," "improve," or even "modernize." And there was enough Republican, conservative, and neocon material floating around for anyone to discover quite easily what specific ideas were in play.

My personal favorite Rosetta Stone was the Texas Republican Party platform. Its declarations are to compassionate conservatism what *Hustler* Online is to *Playboy* magazine. In addition to privatizing Social Security, it calls for privatizing every part of the government that isn't holding a gun. They want to abolish the income tax, the IRS, the Sixteenth Amendment (which created the federal income tax), the inheritance tax—which they are careful to call the "death tax"—corporate income taxes, payroll taxes, and the capital gains tax.

These are to be replaced with a national sales tax.

By the time of Bush's acceptance speech, a bill had already been introduced in the House to do just that. It had fifty-five co-sponsors and the support of House Speaker Dennis Hastert and House Majority Leader Tom DeLay.

The Texas Republicans want "the traditional definition of marriage as a God-ordained, legal and moral commitment only between a natural man and a natural woman," along with a whole variety of antigay legislation, the return of legal corporeal punishment of foster children, prayer in the schools, and the Ten Commandments wherever they can be hung, painted, or placed, in actual tablet form.

Yet neither the media nor the Democratic Party made an issue of Bush's and the Republicans' plans to "transform" Social Security until after Bush was elected and made it a feature of his State of the Union address.

The estimated cost of privatizing Social Security is $2.1 trillion.

Then, in 2005, when Bush presented the budget, the cost of the tax cuts and of privatizing social security were simply left out. As were the costs of the wars in Iraq and Afghanistan.

If this were a movie, the forensic psychologist would say, "He's sending us a message."

And the dull acolyte would say, "What?" with a particularly credulous tone of voice.

The psych would say, gravely, "He's saying stop me! Before I deficit again!"

At which point the dull acolyte looks at the forensic whiz and says, "I don't think so. Look at that smirk and that grin, he's saying, I can't believe they can't catch me."

These are vast numbers. To run up such debts with no plan to pay for them is irresponsible beyond imagining.

To pretend they don't exist, to act as if the bills will never come due, to act as if nobody will notice, and think that you can get away with it is either astonishing bravura or megalomania. Or both.

As a psychiatrist, Justin Frank looks mostly at the beginning years—infancy, the family, and early-childhood years.

My personal experience is that the things we learn as adults, when we go out into the world and see how it actually operates, are equally or more important. Perhaps not to our intimate relationships or our general emotional states, but to the way we function in the public sphere, which is where we spend most of our time.

If we look at Bush's business record, we can see him beginning the kind of behavior he brought to public office, having certain behaviors validated, and picking up new techniques as he goes.

GEORGE BUSH IN BUSINESS

George Bush went into the oil exploration business in 1978. He got millions of dollars from friends of his family. He lost most of it:

> At least $4,700,000 went into Arbusto and its succesor, Bush Exploration. . . . The company returned only $1,500,000 to its investors.

> The *Buying of the President, 2004,* Charles Lewis and
> the Center for Public Integrity

After each failure, people gave him more to lose again.

There were two reasons for that. The first was that oil-exploration companies were tax shelters. If you were rich and had a lot of extra money, we, the people, gave you a free shot at certain long-shot kinds of investments. If you won, you won and got to keep it. If you lost, we'd take the losses off your income tax.

The second reason was that a lot of the investors figured they were really buying political influence when they gave money to George W. Bush.[27] "His name was George Bush. That was worth the money they paid him," Phil Kendrick, the founder of Harken Energy, told *Time* magazine.

George H. W. Bush, Bush's father, had been a congressman, head of CREEP,[28] chairman of the Republican National Committee, and director of the CIA. He was in the midst of running for the Republican nomination for

---

27. The most intriguing connection is James R. Bath. Bath handled other people's money. Among them was Salem bin Laden, Osama's brother. Also

president when George was starting out in business. Bush Sr. would become a two-term VP under Reagan and then a one-term president.

The first company that went broke under Bush was Arbusto, nicknamed "El Busto." He changed the name to Bush Exploration the year his father became vice president. When that went broke, he merged with another company, Spectrum 7. In spite of his track record, the investors put George in charge. Within two years they had $3 million in liabilities and operating losses as high as $400,000 per quarter. They were on the verge of bankruptcy.

To write it off to tax shelters and family friends is to

Khalid bin Mahfouz, an extraordinarily wealthy Saudi who owned a controlling interest in BCCI. BCCI is worth a book in itself. And there are several: *False Profits: The Inside Story of BCCI, the World's Most Corrupt Financial Empire,* by Peter Truell and Larry Gurwin; *The Outlaw Bank: A Wild Ride into the Secret Heart of BCCI,* by Jonathan Beaty; *Dirty Money: BCCI: The Inside Story of the World's Sleaziest Bank,* by Mark Potts, et al.; *Bankrupt: The BCCI Fraud,* by Nick Kochan Bob Whittington.

There was:

fraud by BCCI and BCCI customers involving billions of dollars; money laundering in Europe, Africa, Asia, and the Americas; BCCI's bribery of officials in most of those locations; its support of terrorism, arms trafficking, and the sale of nuclear technologies; its management of prostitution; its commission and facilitation of income tax evasion, smuggling, and illegal immigration; its illicit purchases of banks and real estate; and a panoply of financial crimes limited only by the imagination of its officers and customers.

Among BCCI's principal mechanisms for committing crimes were shell corporations, bank confidentiality and secrecy havens, layering of corporate structure, front-men and nominees, back-to-back financial documentation among BCCI controlled entities, kick-backs and bribes, intimidation of witnesses, and retention of well-placed insiders to discourage governmental action.

A Report to the Committee on Foreign Relations, United States
Senate, by Senator John Kerry and Senator Hank Brown,
December 1992, 102d Congress 2d Session Senate Print 102-140

misunderestimate George. To lose $6 million, almost never make a profit, and still have people come back to you and like you and put you in positions of responsibility and give you additional large sums of money—that takes a great deal of talent.

It is a salesman's talent. It involves a certain brave optimism. Or shamelessness. Depending on the day and the quality of the product you actually have to sell. If the product is not the best and the most aboveboard, it calls for some nondisclosure and misrepresentation. If you're going to stay out of trouble, you need to be able to do that without the sort of outright lies that will get lawyers involved. Bush seems to have had the knack

Then, in 1987, along came:

HARKEN ENERGY

Harken specialized in buying distressed oil companies. Which was not an entirely bad idea. The oil business was at the bottom of one of its boom-and-bust cycles. A lot of companies were genuinely undervalued.

But to follow connections to BCCI is to fall down the rabbit hole of conspiracy theory and perhaps never come out.

It will take you, among other places, to Bert Lance, the banker who backed Jimmy Carter, and to the wildest of the rumors that swirled around Bill Clinton: CIA cocaine operations in Mena, Arkansas, killings that he covered up as governor and the "murder" of Vince Foster.

In case you missed it, the Senate report was by John Kerry. So we already have Bush, Kerry, and the bin Ladens crossing paths, and if that's not enough, one of the major investors in Harken Energy before George Bush came aboard was George Soros.

28. The most apt acronym in history, Nixon's Committee to Re-Elect the President. All sorts of untracked cash went in and the dirty deeds came out, including the Watergate burglary and the cover-up

Bush was made a company director, for which he got $2,000 per meeting, and a consultant, at a salary that went from $85,000 up to $120,000 per year and then down to $45,000. He got 200,000 shares of Harken, worth "at least $500,000." All of that, and "it was not a full time job."[29]

Does it get any better than that?

Yes, it does. Bush also got options to buy shares at 40 percent of their value. And Harken would lend him the money to take advantage of the offer. At insider rates. He later availed himself of that opportunity, borrowed $180,000, bought the shares, and then asked that the loan be changed to a nonrecourse loan, meaning that if he didn't pay it back, well, too bad, he didn't have to. Next time you're speaking to the folks who own the paper on your car or your house, ask them if they would like to change your loan to a nonrecourse loan. When they say no, have them explain why not.

Would that all of our failures would end up so happily.

After George Bush joined Harken, new investors showed up. These included Harvard Management Group, which handles Harvard University's endowment. They had never invested in Texas oil exploration before. In terms of exercising fiduciary responsibility, why they would do so now and why they would choose Harken as a place to start seems, at first glance, incomprehensible. They initially put in $20 million. They put in a great deal more later on.

Then Jackson Stephens, a Little Rock, Arkansas, billionaire, got involved. Stephens was also a major backer of Bill Clinton. Stephens hooked Harken up with Union Bank of

29. Byron York, "The Facts about Bush and Harken: The President's Story Holds Up Under Scrutiny," *New Republic,* July 10, 1992.

Switzerland. George Bush was at the meeting where that was discussed.[30] UBS bought 5 percent of Harken through a bank that was a joint venture between itself and BCCI. (Robert Gates, the director of the CIA under George H. W. Bush, liked to call BCCI "the bank of crooks and criminals international.")

Two years after Bush arrived, Harken was in trouble. They were going to have to report losses of at least $12,566,000.

They didn't want to.

Keep your eye on the cards. There's one red card, two black cards. Watch them, it's easy to follow . . . see that guy . . . he just won, doubled his money . . . now you try it . . . anybody can do it . . . keep your eye on the red queen . . . Aloha . . .

ALOHA

Harken owned Aloha Petroleum, a gas-station chain in Hawaii. It was on their books as being worth $5.1 million.

Several of the directors of Harken formed a company. Harken lent them $11 million. That loan would be collateralized only by Aloha, once they purchased it. They added $1,000,000 and used the $12,000,000 to buy 80 percent of Aloha.

On its quarterly statement of earnings, Harken now claimed to have 20 percent of Aloha, valued at $1 million, plus $1 million in cash from the sale, plus $11 million owed to them by the company the insiders had formed, for a total of $13 million.

One asset worth $5.1 million had become $13 million, thereby increasing the value of Harken by $7,900,000.

30. According to Louis Dubose, Julie Hollar, and Nate Blakeslee, "Dubya and the Press," *Texas Observer,* September 17, 1999, available online at texasobserver.org/showArticle.asp?ArticleID=264.

So instead of reporting a $12.5 million loss, they reported a loss of just $3.3 million.

BAHRAIN

In the Persian Gulf east of Saudi Arabia, which has the largest oil reserves in the world, and just north of Qatar, which has the largest offshore natural-gas fields in the world, is the archipelago of Bahrain, a small country with a population of 677,000.

In 1990, Bahrain gave Harken Energy exclusive rights to explore its offshore territories for oil and gas.

It became the talk of the oil business. Amoco, among others, had been trying to get the contract. Harken was a relatively small organization; a hodge-podge of acquisitions of failed companies, with incomprehensible books, bad cash flow, no offshore drilling experience, and without sufficient capital even to start the job.

Harken claims never to have sought the contract. George Bush claims to have opposed it.

In spite of Bahrain's tempting location, it was a long shot. They had not had a significant find since 1932, and it was not for want of trying.

But it certainly made Harken look like they were players.

Which they needed to do. Because they were continuing to lose money.

Harken had been planning to raise money by going public.

On May 8, 1990, Harken was advised by Smith Barney that "until the Company restructured its equity situation and resolved it's restrictive covenants with its banks, . . . there was no potential for it to raise equity money through a public offering." Which is investment underwriter speak for: You owe so much and the banks are so on top of you for it that nobody is gonna give you a nickel.

On May 20, Harken officials warned the board that the company was going to run out of cash and was "already technically in default at that point."

They got another bank to take over the loans.

Then, "at the July 1990 board meeting, Mr. Bush and other directors decided to "establish a 'joint venture' with Harvard Management."[31]

A SHORT DIGRESSION FOR A WONDERFUL AND
INSTRUCTIVE STORY

Most accounts of Harvard Management's participation in Harken Energy make it sound both foolish and mysterious. These writers presume, without being explicit about it, that the Harvard fund managers were staid Easterners who were used to carefully husbanding a university endowment and that someone or something must have gotten into their tea and they went briefly mad and lost a ton of money in the wild and woolly world of Texas wildcatting.

Harvard Watch, which has done a marvelous job of digging into the endowment and how it has been managed, points out that two people from Harvard were on the Harken board of directors. They personally held shares in Harken.

Together, the Harvard and Harken people came up with the following plan. They created a new entity, Aneas Venture Corporation, or AVC. Harken "sold" Aneas several of its subsidiaries that were carrying large debts in

31. Glen R. Simpson, "Harvard Was Unlikely Savior of Bush Energy Firm Harken," *Wall Street Journal,* October 9, 2002.

return for equity in the new company. This moved the debts off Harken's books. In addition, AVC contracted to pay Harken substantial management fees. This made it look as if Harken had income and cash flow.

Harken's shares had fallen to $1.25 in late 1990. But when the Harvard-AVC deals went through in 1991, making their financial picture look so much better, the stock climbed to $8 a share.

Harvard Management sold 1.6 million shares between September 1991 and October 1992. They made quite a lot of money. So, presumably, did the managers who held seats on Harken's board.

Afterward, reality was allowed to take over again. Harken shares began their slow decline from the $6.50 range to between two and four cents a share. (If you look it up, it may look like twenty and forty, but there was a one-for-ten stock swap in there).

In August 1990, before the Harvard deals went into effect, Harken reported a loss of $23 million for the quarter.

But by July—after that meeting, but before the August statement—George Bush had bailed out.

He sold his stock for $4 a share, a total of $848,560. When the August statement came out, the stock went down to $2.37 a share. At which price he would only have made $502,771. A difference of $345,788.

Was that insider trading?

There was a letter from Harken's lawyers that came just before Bush sold his shares. It warned insiders that if they knew anything detrimental to the company that outsiders would not know, they were advised not to sell.

George Bush was on the board of directors and on the audit committee. He received "flash" reports, updates of the company's financial condition, between statements. He had been informed that the company was going to run out of cash. He was in a position to know that the Aloha deal was flimflam. He was part of the group that planned the bailout with Harvard. Did George Bush know that Harken Energy was in worse shape than the public would have known prior to the August 1990 statement that said they were $23 million in the hole?

He says he didn't have a clue. That he got the lawyers to sign off on his stock sale and he thought it was all fine and proper.

Not only that: "The SEC fully investigated the stock deal," George Bush said. "I was exonerated."

Actually a letter from the SEC to Bush's attorneys said, "The investigation has been terminated as to the conduct of Mr. Bush, and . . . at this time, no enforcement action is contemplated with respect to him. . . . [This] must in no way be construed as indicating that the party has been exonerated or that no action may ultimately result."

The SEC investigation appears to have come about because Bush had not filed the forms an insider is supposed to file when he sells his stock.

The chairman of the SEC, Richard Breeden, was a Bush Sr. appointment. Before that, he had been an economic policy adviser to President Bush. Before that, he had been a partner in the law firm Baker Botts, James Baker's law firm.

James Baker is to the Bush family what Tom Hagen was to the Corleone family. In saying this I mean no disrespect.

The SEC's general counsel was James Doty. He was also from Baker Botts. The reason George Bush had sold his Harken stock was to pay for his stake in the Texas Rangers baseball team. James Doty had been George Bush's lawyer on that end of the deal.

There are two more details worth noting.

The SEC never questioned Bush or any of the other partners.

The letter from the lawyers that warned against insider trades was not delivered to the SEC until the day after the investigation was closed. It did not come to light until 2002.[32]

BUSH FIGURES OUT HOW TO MAKE MONEY

Bush sold his shares in Harken to pay off the loan he had gotten to participate in buying the Texas Rangers baseball team. A deal he put together.

MISUNDERESTIMATING

George is sort of given credit for putting together the Texas Rangers deal or at least for spearheading it. But then we are reminded that he couldn't quite put it together himself and had to have others come in, the big dogs with the big bones and the big bucks, and they really nailed it:

> In a pattern repeated through his business career, Mr. Bush's play did not quite make the grade. Baseball Commissioner Peter Ueberroth stepped in, brokering a deal that brought Fort Worth financier Richard Rainwater together with the Bush group. Mr. Ueberroth's

32. Peter Behr, "Bush Sold Stock after Lawyers' Warning; SEC Closed Probe before Receiving Letter from Harken's Outside Attorneys," *Washington Post,* November 1, 2002.

pitch to Mr. Rainwater was that he join the deal partly "out of respect" for President Bush, a source close to the negotiations told the *New York Times*.

Wall Street Journal, September 18, 1999, p. A26

Once the deal went through, and they bought the team, George was depicted as the figurehead.

He was the guy who would sit by the dugout every day, rooting for the team, eating pumpkin seeds. He did the press conferences and got out on the stump, boosterizing. The "business" was presumably run by someone else.

Even when he had his own companies, the situations are described as if he were some guy who drifted through with some money from his family connections, who promptly lost it and then got more, because his name remained the same as his father's.

I think that's Bush's style. And a brilliant and deceptive one it is. He always walks away making money. It always looks like pure luck. That helps when there's blame to pass around. No one sends the leg breakers or even the lawyers after George. Neither law enforcement nor the media think of him as responsible for any of the shady acts that may have taken place while he was on the board of directors and the audit committee, because he's just there for his name.

Later on, when he beat political opponent after political opponent, it was Karl Rove who had to be Bush's "brain." When he got to the White House, it had to be Dick Cheney who was running things:

our president is not an imbecile but an operator just as canny as he is hard-hearted—which is to say he is extraordinarily shrewd. To smirk at his alleged stupidity is, therefore, not just to miss the point, but to do this unelected president a giant favor.

The Bush Dsylexicon: Observations on a National Disorder, Mark Crispin Miller (Norton, 2002), p. 2

It has been a great trap for his opponents all through his career. Especially people on the left who tend to revere a "literate" style so much that they confuse that style with intelligence itself. Indeed, just as the right-wing critics of the academic and media elites claim, those elites do have contempt for unliterate styles of smarts. The literature professor looks down on the car dealer, however rich. The artist looks down on the businessperson, even as he asks for a grant. The woman with the Ph.D. looks down on the football coach. And all of them are baffled when Dwight Eisenhower, Ronald Reagan, and George W. Bush get to be president. And then get re-elected.

I maintain that nobody gets to be president without being very, very smart.

When we evaluate his business career, even though it is filled with bankruptcies, that should be kept in mind.

The first thing that Bush's group did when they took over the team was threaten to move it, the now-standard ploy to force the city to finance a new stadium.

The city of Arlington agreed to come up with $135,000,000. The owners were to put up $55,000,000, which they were going to earn back through a surcharge on baseball tickets.

Then they could buy the stadium for $60,000,000.

They paid $5,000,000 a year in rent. The rent could be applied to the purchase price. After twelve years, the stadium was theirs. For nothing, except having paid rent.[33] If you are a renter, I recommend that you speak to your landlord as soon as possible. Show him this arrangement and see if you can make a similar deal.

The city raised its share of the money through an increase in the sales tax. For every two dollars Mom spent when she went shopping for groceries, she tossed in a penny for the new stadium.

The team, on the other hand, got exemptions from various sales and property taxes.

The deal included the land on which the old Arlington Stadium and its parking lot sat, but the group also wanted an additional 200 acres for commercial development. So the state legislature created the Arlington Sports Facilities Development Authority for them. Its had the power of eminent domain, the ability to force landowners to sell their property. In the days before he learned message discipline, George Bush told the *Forth Worth Star-Telegram*, "The idea of making a land play, absolutely, to plunk the field down in the middle of a big piece of land, that's kind of always been the strategy."

---

33. "George's Road to Riches," Byron York, *American Spectator,* 1999. Talk about fog facts. I must have read two dozen accounts of this deal, and only one other mentioned this detail of the applied rent being the entirety of the purchase price. It was in Worse Than Watergate: The Secret Presidency of George W. Bush, by John W. Dean. The footnote there led me to York's original.

Another detail that appeared only in York's piece was the number of extra acres that the team owners got to seize for commercial development while they were building the stadium.

Nobody has published a figure on how much those land deals made for the group. But not only was the team able to force people to sell, they were able to force the prices so low that when several of the ex-landowners sued, the court awarded them $22,200,000. The Bush group never paid. They just ignored the judgment. It was only paid after the team was sold, by the new ownership.

Ostensibly, Bush got involved in the team so as to be become a public personality from which to launch a political career. As if it wasn't about the money. It was just about sitting in the dugout and cheering and being on TV.

In 1994, Bush ran for governor of Texas and won. He put all his assets in a blind trust. Except his interest in the team.

Bush had learned from Harvard and Harken what could be done with the huge sums of money in a university endowment. In 1996, as governor, Bush established the University of Texas Investment Management Company (UTIMCO). This privatized the University of Texas's endowment. That endowment was nine billion dollars ($9,000,000,000). UTIMCO also got control of the University's land and oil holdings, another seven and a half billion dollars ($7,500,000,000).

Unlike the Board of Regents, which had previously controlled the money, UTIMCO was not required to hold open meetings or publish its activities. If the man in charge wanted to treat it like a giant slush fund to reward his friends and enrich himself, he certainly could.

The man Bush put in charge of all these billions was Thomas Hicks.

In 1996 Thomas Hicks returned the favor. He bought the Texas Rangers for $250 million—almost three times what Bush's group had paid for it.

On first glance that appears to be a terrific profit. Any

true-believing capitalist would say, hey, if they increased the value of the team that much, they damn well deserve it. Or even if they simply had the foresight to catch the wave of the rise in the value of sports franchises in general, they deserve it. That's what being a businessman is all about: you take the risks, you reap the rewards.

It's worth a second look.

Cost of the franchise	$89,000,000
Cost of the new stadium	$190,000,000[34]
Total:	$279,000,000
Sale of the team	$250,000,000
Cost of the team	$279,000,000
Actual increase in value	($29,000,000)

There is actually a $29,000,000 loss.

So $29,000,000 of value had . . . gone missing. But who cared? The Bush group had gotten their money back, plus whatever they made on the 200 extra commercial acres, plus whatever they made operating the team, plus $161,000,000.

The bottom line was that they got $135,000,000 from the people of Arlington, at the rate of half a cent for every dollar they spent on their daily expenses, plus $26,000,000, raised a dollar at time on every ticket sold to the fans, and they lost $29,000,000. Thomas Hicks was happy. He got a $279 million package for just $250 million. Hicks went on to become a Pioneer (big Bush fund-raiser) and vice chairman of Clear Channel Communications, an important corporate supporter of Bush.

34. Reported elsewhere as $189,000,000, also as $191,000,000 and sometimes as $135,000,000 plus $55,000,000.

Bush had put in $600,000. His share was increased beyond his financial contribution for reasons that still remain obscure but that included a bonus if the sale of the team netted back the full investment plus interest.

His share of the deal was $13 million.

And that's how George Bush got rich.

HOW DICK CHENEY GOT RICH

A poor boy from Wyoming goes to Washington. He spends almost his whole life working for the public on a government salary and ends up worth at least forty-four million dollars ($44,000,000).

It's a real Horatio Alger story.

A GRAND LITERARY DIGRESSION

The standard usage of Horatio Alger's name is an exercise in delusion.

By leading exemplary lives, struggling valiantly against poverty and adversity, Alger's heroes gain wealth and honor.

Columbia Encyclopedia, 6th ed., online

inspirational adventure stories for boys; virtue and hard work overcome poverty.

thefreedictionary.com

the spirit of Strive and Succeed . . . undaunted heroes—lads whose struggles epitomized the great American dream and inspired heroic ideals in countless millions of young Americans.

The Horatio Alger Society

Horatio Alger (1834–1899) wrote about 130 short novels. Like the Hardy Boys and Nancy Drew, which I read at the same age, they are all the same, yet all quite readable. Alger had a great gift for narrative. For some reason or other, I happened to pick one up as an adult. I was quite surprised at what I was reading. Then I read several more to see if that was an aberration. No, that part of my memory, at least, was correct; they are all exactly the same.

They feature a boy just at, or on the verge of, puberty, from the country or the slums. He comes to the center of the big city. He does work, but he doesn't work astonishingly hard, certainly not as compared to the majority of other working children in the days of legal child labor. He doesn't start his own business or invent a better mousetrap or find the Northwest Passage.

What really happens is he meets a rich older man who takes quite a fancy to him and sets him up with money and educates him and teaches him how to dress and conduct himself.

There is, indeed, a "meet cute" in which the boy does something that draws that nice rich man's attention. It's usually something heroic, like stopping a team of galloping horses that's dragging a coach that is carrying the rich man's daughter.

This action is referred to in the books themselves and by

people like those at the Horatio Alger Society as a sign of character. It is also a chance for the older man to notice how this boy stands out from the other boys. He has that forth-right, noble-boy quality. Which is very, very attractive. Eager, earnest, shining. It's what draws priests to alter boys. In addition to the convenience, of course.

I do not understand how an adult can read Alger's stories and not realize that these were homosexual pedophile fantasies. Actually, it's a single fantasy repeated over and over again.

So I looked him up. And there it was. He had started out as a minister in Brewster, Massachusetts. He was having sex with boys in his congregation. Two of them told their parents. He admitted to a certain "practice." He resigned and moved to New York City. There he became a writer and began churning out these fantasies as dime novels.

We have two distinct ideas of what happened when he went to New York. Jessica Amanda Salmonson, a critic, antiquarian bookseller, and gay activist, has written: "Alger continued his 'practice' although thereafter most often against types of boys nobody cared about, thus avoiding fur-ther trouble with authorities. The newsboys Alger glamor-ized in his fiction were in reality homeless child laborers who spent their nights in alleys or slum-squats. . . . Their plight included sexual exploitation ranging from outright rape to 'willing' prostitution."[35]

Stefan Kanfer, writing in the *City Journal*, a publication of the Manhattan Institute, a neoconservative propaganda

35. Salmonson, "The Dark Side of Horatio Alger, Jr.," www.violetbooks.com/alger.html.

mill,[36] has a very different tale to tell: "The fugitive repaired to New York City in the spring of 1866. Though never to wear the cloth again, he resolved to live out the Christian ideal, expiating his sin by saving others."

Upon seeing the slum children of New York, "an idea came to him. . . . He had sinned against youths; now he would rescue them and in the process save himself. He would do it as a novelist."

In this version, Alger never had sex with a young boy again (nor anyone, presumably, as there is no reference to marriages, mistresses, or an adult male companion). Kanfer describes also how Alger did many good works, works that kept him close to the youngsters he was trying to save, and how he helped many of them and found them places with his friends.[37]

So, two distinct interpretations of Alger's reality.

On the one hand we have the gay activist saying, in essence, "Let's get real. Alger was a sexual predator, and sexual predators stay sexual predators. Going to the big cities was the sexual tourism of the day. There were plenty of young girls and boys with no means of support and you could buy what you can buy in Bangkok today."

Kanfer comes out fighting for hypocrisy.

Elsewhere, George Bush, in a series of private conversations that were taped by a friend, explained the reasoning for hypocrisy over honesty as a policy choice:

---

36. It refers to itself as a think tank whose mission is to "disseminate new ideas that foster greater economic choice and individual responsibility."

37. In his will, Alger instructed his sister, Augusta, to destroy his diary and all his personal correspondence. In 1927, Herbert Mayes was hired to write a biography. Not only were there no papers, but none of Alger's contemporaries would talk about him.

Mr. Bush said [to Mr. Wead]: "'I wouldn't answer the marijuana questions. You know why? Because I don't want some little kid doing what I tried.'"

He mocked Vice President Al Gore for acknowledging marijuana use. "Baby boomers have got to grow up and say, yeah, I may have done drugs, but instead of admitting it, say to kids, don't do them," he said.[38]

Joe Conason, in the *New York Observer* wrote, "For many American parents of a certain age, that self-serving yet poignant response must strike an empathetic chord. Concern that children will mimic parental misbehavior is universal, and so is the impulse to conceal embarrassing truths."

Hypocrisy of this type, though not labeled as such, is part of the Republican Party's program and has a great deal do with its appeal.

In the constellation of Republicanism, conservatism, and Christianity, the source of order is authority.[39] A choice, a statement, or a rule is not made valid by logic or proof or evidence. It comes from the authority of the source. A godly man gets it from the ministers of God, who get it from the Bible, which is the word of God himself.

If there is no "authority," then there will be no order.

To preserve order, therefore, we need to believe that each link in the chain is unbroken. To do so requires an effort not to know certain things.

In the matter of Horatio Alger's novels, this is probably

38. In "Secretly Taped Conversations, Glimpses of the Future President," by David D. Kirkpatrick, New York Times, February 20, 2005.

39. A gross generality. But, as a group with a group psychology, they lean that way and certainly they campaign that way.

trivial. But when it applies to abstinence-only sex education, it leads to unwanted teen pregnancies and increased transmission of STDs, and it brings misery and death. When it applies to not doing stem cell research, it perpetuates disease, pain, and early death.

Once we accept and sanction hypocrisy in matters of sexual morality, drinking, and doing drugs, the act of saying one thing and doing another becomes the norm in all things.

The president wanted to take out Saddam Hussein because he was evil. It's good to oppose evil. In order to convince the world to go along, it was necessary to make a specific claim. So he said that Saddam had weapons of mass destruction and he was linked to terrorism and that's linked to Al Qaeda. When those specific claims turn out to be false, that's alright, because the hypocritical form—say what is necessary to do God's will and oppose evil, true or not—is the accepted form.

Here was a fog. The myth of Horatio Alger.

To get to the facts, we did something relatively simple. We ignored the rhetoric and looked at the events. Which is sort of funny, since, in this case, they're both fiction. Still, if we stripped the rhetoric off the facts and they stood naked, we saw them for what they were.

Then we looked outside. In this case, to the author's life. There was a correspondence. He was, in real life, the character who appears in every book, under different names and in different guises, the outwardly reputable older man—a pastor, no less—who is very fond of young boys.

This is, intellectually, relatively easy to do.

It is socially and psychologically difficult. Our social and psychological methods of sorting out the world will generally trump our strictly intellectual ones. There are certain automatics that exist in almost any situation. We automatically give credence to what people tell us. We give additional respect to the words of people in authority. We tend to go with the group. We compartmentalize. We let our preachers preach, our leaders lead and Click and Clack, the Tappet Brothers, fix our cars. These things are neither good nor bad. They are efficient and they bring personal and social benefits.

Here, there were additional factors.

Alger's rhetoric creates fog. There are clean and noble boys and there are adult men, whose motives are good and pure, who help such boys. Teachers and coaches and librarians and Scout leaders and even priests do reach out to young people and enter into asexual mentor-protégé relationships without groping them, and help them find their way. That's good and it is necessary and it is a significant part of social life.

So there could be truth in it. Certainly there ought to be truth in it.

The preaching about being good and godly and all the rest in Alger's novels sounds sincere. So does his poem, *Friar Anselmo's Sin,* which is taken to be autobiographical, is full of regret and repentance and is about the promise of redemption through good deeds:

> Courage, Anselmo, though thy sin be great,
> God grants thee life that thou may'st expiate.
>
> Thy guilty stains shall be washed white again,
> By noble service done thy fellow-men.

Alger reportedly did do good deeds and helped out many a young man.

This last is only marred by our suspicion that pedophiles who choose to work in positions that keep them in contact with youngsters, have ulterior motives, or, at the very least are placing themselves nearer to temptation than they ought to.

Alger's sincerity and his confiscation of the sort of truths that we are fond of confuse us.

At the very least, if he is sincere, then he is not a liar. To be a liar requires intentionality. To accuse someone of being a liar means that we are saying that they are aware of the difference between reality and the things they say and that they are making a choice to deceive.

This mix—predatory desires cloaked in the rhetoric of goodness, sincerity so sincere, we can't believe it's not genuine, statements that could be real, even should be real, but aren't, untruths that we are hard-pressed to call lies—can exist in other, completely nonsexual contexts.

We don't have words for that. We don't have a label that describes the sort of people who speak such untruths with such sincerity from within such delusions.

The name of the New York chapter of NAMBLA, the North American Man Boy Love Association, is the Horatio Alger Chapter.

* * *

The question was: How did a man who spent his life in public service end up with $44 million?

Under George Bush the First, Dick Cheney was secretary of defense.

I don't know why. He had no military experience or

expertise. When he had the chance to fight, he fought to be deferred from the draft, over and over again, until he was too old to be called up for service. T. D. Allman summed it up neatly in *Rolling Stone* ("The Curse of Dick Cheney," August 25, 2004):

> First he enrolled in Casper Community College; then he went to the University of Wyoming. That kept him out of the draft until August 7th, 1964, when Congress initiated massive conscription in the armed forces. Three weeks later, Cheney married Lynne Vincent, his childhood girlfriend, earning him another deferment. Then on October 26th, 1965, the Selective Service announced that childless married men no longer would be exempted from having to fight for their country. Nine months and two days later, the first of Cheney's two daughters, Elizabeth, was born. All told, between 1963 and 1966, Cheney received five deferments.

As secretary of defense, he commissioned a study on privatizing the armed forces. He hired Halliburton to do that study and a follow-up. Together the studies cost $8,900,000. And were classified. Cheney decided he liked Halliburton's ideas. He chose Halliburton to implement Halliburton's recommendations. He gave the company contracts to do all of the military's support work for the next five years. The contracts had guaranteed profits.

George Bush the First failed to get reelected.

The contracts lived on.

Cheney had to go to work in the private sector. He had been in the public sector for twenty-four years. His only previous nongovernmental experience had been working on a telephone company repair crew in Wyoming for two years after he dropped out of Yale, apparently flunking too many of his courses.

He started his own PAC. Supposedly he was considering a run for president. It is hard to imagine this slouched, sneering, smirking, pale, lumpy man with a serious heart condition making a serious run for the presidency in the television age. No matter, the PAC allowed corporations to give him money, Halliburton among them. In October 1993, Halliburton suddenly hired him as their chief executive officer. His salary was in the $2 million range, he got houses and cars and jets and unlimited expense money for food and parties and travel. He also got stock in the company.

There are two ways to look at this: that Cheney was an extremely talented man, with lots of contacts but no business experience or; that it was an after-the-fact payoff. In the nineteenth century Tammany bagmen got their name by delivering cash in brown paper bags, like money was tuna on rye wrapped in wax paper, with a pickle. That's not how it's done nowadays. Instead the payoff comes by stepping through the revolving door, from the side of public duty and protecting the common good to the side of gold and gain and getting as much you can. And sometimes back again.

Cheney did in fact have lots of influence with many governments and he got lots of government contracts for Halliburton. But his decisions as head of the company were so bad that they drove Halliburton to the verge of bankruptcy. In 2003 two of the company's subsidiaries finally did have to file for Chapter 11.

As CEO of Halliburton, Cheney presided over a change to "Enron-style" accounting methods that counted "probable" collections on cost overruns. These accounting procedures were not by themselves illegal. But failure to notify shareholders that the change had been made was. Regulators called it "materially misleading." This led to shareholder lawsuits, a suit by Judicial Watch,[40] and an investigation by the SEC.

The Judicial Watch lawsuit, similar to the shareholder suits, alleged that "Halliburton overstated revenues by $445 million from 1999 though the end of 2001. The Judicial Watch lawsuit was dismissed. They are considering an appeal. Halliburton settled the shareholder lawsuits for about $6 million.

The SEC investigation was settled with a $7.5 million penalty payment on August 3, 2004.

Also, while Cheney was CEO, Halliburton subsidiaries did business with Libya, Iran, and Iraq, all on the terrorist watch list. Cheney categorically denied doing business with Iraq.

Cheney's biggest single mistake as CEO of Halliburton was the acquisition of Halliburton's chief rival, Dresser Industries. He overlooked their asbestos liabilities.

It's worth taking a detour here into the fog of asbestos litigation.

To the average person this asbestos business is something of a mystery. It used to be a normal building material; now, suddenly, men in white suits have to come and dispose of it, and evil litigators are costing companies millions with their class action suits.

---

40. Judicial Watch is generally considered a conservative group. It went after both Bill and Hillary Clinton.

Asbestos judgments are high for a reason. It is not merely because asbestos gives people dreadful, debilitating diseases and then kills them. It's because the asbestos companies knew it and they worked avidly, just like the tobacco companies, to cover up that information and to convince the world their product was safe.

Way back in 1919, the Prudential Insurance Company stopped selling insurance to asbestos workers. In 1928, researchers established exactly how asbestos got into the tissue of the lungs and caused disease. Yet the industry cover-up was so successful that right up through the 1970s, high school science classes taught that asbestos was a harmless and useful building material. It was fireproofing material; it made us *safer*.

When you explain that to juries, many of whom have lived in homes and worked in offices and gone to schools filled with asbestos, then juries give out awards.

These awards are not very large individually. Mesothelioma victims don't get to spend their final years of agony on Paradise Island, basking by the pool at their private villas and chauffeured to the casinos where their personal servants push them in their wheelchairs and maintain their morphine drips.

But they are huge in the aggregate, so huge as to threaten several companies, like Halliburton, with bankruptcy.

Those who cry for tort reform always complain that the lawyers are getting rich. But it is the attempt to get rich that is supposed to create "good" in a free-market system. The lawyers, seeking their own profit, get money for the medical care of the people injured through dangerous and deceptive practices. That puts the cost on the people who did the wrong, rather than spreading it around unfairly, like universal health care would do. If the cost is high enough, it will hopefully serve as a deterrent the next time a company wants to hide the fact that its product or its process kills people.

Thus we see how it is good to be sued.

Facts become visible through context and framing. Sometimes we don't bother to frame things or refer to the context because it seems too basic and too obvious.

ECONOMICS 101: CAPITALISM

IT IS THE PURPOSE OF A BUSINESS TO MAKE MONEY

If a business sells you a product or a service, it wants to charge you as much as it can and give you as little as it can, produced at the lowest cost at which it can produce it.

With insurance or pensions or any other kind of investment, it is to the advantage of the businesses to get you to put in as much as possible and then to pay out at little as possible.

That is the moral and ethical and legal imperative of the people running that business. If they knowingly do otherwise, they are liable to their investors.

In a short-run situation, an insurance company that takes in premiums and never pays benefits, like the one depicted in John Grisham's *The Rainmaker*, is an ideal business.

In the long term, reputation, consumer knowledge, and competition become factors.

If enough people find out that the company does not pay out on claims, eventually they will stop signing up and go elsewhere. Provided there is an elsewhere and they have an affordable choice.

In the short run, there is only law and regulation.

The short run can occur at any time.

For example: Highlands Insurance.

Highlands was Halliburton's own health-insurance company, formed in 1950, to cover its many workers. Why pay all those premiums to someone else? Halliburton is primarily in the construction business. It used a lot of asbestos. As with smoking, asbestos diseases take twenty or thirty years—or even more—to show up.

That's one of the complications of compensating asbestos victims. The original company is often gone. The original management certainly is. So a new entity, or at least new management, is facing an old liability that it might not have known was coming and that it feels is unfair, since it did not commit the wrong. But that, too, is the way property works in a capitalist system. Liabilities and assets both travel with the company through time.

In 1995, when Dick Cheney became the new CEO of Halliburton, the company's lawyers informed him that they were worried that asbestos-related illnesses were showing up and that could pose a problem for Highlands.

Cheney decided to do something very similar to what happened at Harken. He decided to spin Highland off and make it a separate company, and gave Halliburton shareholders shares in the new company. He told them that the deal would be good for both companies:

> Documents generated by Halliburton, a Dallas-based oil services and construction firm, describing the deal to Highlands investors, revealed trivial items that insur-

ance executives would lose in the spin-off, such as voice mail, computers, use of the Halliburton aircraft, and access to its hunting lodge near Houston and a fishing facility in Duck Key, Fla.

They did not mention a huge potential liability for worker asbestos injuries that was looming as Highlands launched its independent business, taking along Halliburton as a major customer. Within a few years of the spinoff, Highlands found itself saddled with 23,000 claims worth about $80 million from workers at a major Halliburton subsidiary, Brown & Root. By 2000, the weight of the claims pushed the publicly traded Highlands into deep financial trouble.

> "Cheney's Role Questioned in Company's Asbestos
> Claims," James V. Grimaldi, *Washington Post*,
> Monday, August 19, 2002

It ended up in court with both sides refusing to pay the claims.

Neither side fought to make sure that the human beings who had damaged their health while building things for Halliburton got their medical care paid for. The few news stories on the litigation and the background events which led to it, that made it out of the fog, didn't even mention what happened to them.

One of the primary goals of this administration is tort reform. A tort is a civil wrong for which the law may supply a remedy. Tort reform is packaged as protecting your local OBGYN, so he or she won't be afraid to deliver babies.

In reality, it will do a great deal more to protect large industrial companies.

Companies like Halliburton, which incurred liabilities through their conduct—exposing workers to asbestos—and bad business decisions—deciding to self-insure and buying another company with asbestos liabilities.

We have a system in which regulation is weak and getting weaker. There has rarely, if ever, been a fine for misconduct so large that it exceeded the additional profit made by breaking the rules. Suing is the only system we have in place to get recompense when a person is injured by a corporation that poisons the water or the air or that sells tainted food, by automobiles that explode, by products that poison children, or by drugs that destroy one of your organs or cause premature death as a side effect, even though the companies had cause to know it would happen.

Even, oh, for the romantic days of classical capitalism, when businessmen were risk-takers! Now, alas, it is being replaced by Bush-Cheneyism, where businessmen get the government to come in and cover for their mistakes.

Cheney likes to be mysterious. How much money does he have? In 2002, CBS News said that it was "between $19.1 and $86.4 million."[41]

When he left Halliburton in 2000, Cheney told Larry King, "What happens financially, obviously, is I take a bath, in one sense."

However, according to the *New York Times* (August 12, 2000) he retired "with a package worth an estimated $20 million, according to people who have reviewed the deal."

Cheney said, in September 2003 on NBC, that "I've severed all my ties with the company, gotten rid of all my

41. cbsnews.com/stories/2003/09/26/politics/main575356.shtml.

financial interest. I have no financial interest in Halliburton of any kind and haven't had, now, for over three years."

According to Factcheck, he did receive a check from Halliburton for $1,452,398 dated two days before he took office on January 20, 2001, and $147,579 earlier in the month.[42] He continues to receive deferred compensation of about $150,000 per year. This is close to his salary of $186,300 a year as vice president.

Cheney retains stock options on 433,333 shares, which would be $18,000,000 at $43 a share.[43] He has pledged to give all after-tax profits to charities should he exercise the options, though it seems to me that if he really wanted to claim that he had severed all ties, he simply could have given the options to charities and let them exercise them or, if the conditions of the options did not permit that, simply renounced them.

In 2000, Dick and Lynn Cheney claimed an adjusted gross income of $36,086,635 on their tax return, according to a White House press release.

The big money came from selling stock:

When Cheney left Halliburton in August 2000 to be Bush's running mate, the oil-services firm was swelling with profits and approaching a two-year high in its stock price. Investors and the public (and possibly Cheney himself) did not know how sick the company really was, as became evident in the months after Cheney left.

Whether through serendipity or shrewdness, Cheney made an $18.5 million profit selling his shares for more

42. factcheck.org/article261.html.

43. The approximate price as this was being written in May, 2005.

than $52 each in August 2000; 60 days later, the company surprised investors with a warning that its engineering and construction business was doing much worse than expected, driving shares down 11 percent in a day. About the same time, it announced it was under a grand jury investigation for overbilling the government.

In the months that followed, it became clear that Halliburton's liability for asbestos claims, stemming from a company Cheney acquired in 1998, were far greater than Halliburton realized. Then, in May of this year, the company announced it was under investigation by the Securities and Exchange Commission for controversial accounting under Cheney's leadership that inflated profits. Halliburton shares closed at $13.10 yesterday on the New York Stock Exchange.[44]

There's the choice. Either it was insider trading or he was blind to what was immediately coming up for his company. An interesting track record for the man that so many people say is really running the country.

These are important stories. They have their complexities, their twists and turns, but they are fairly clear. If they had been told, clearly and simply, we might have known what Bush and Cheney's economic policies and practices would be like once they got hold of an entire country.

If those narratives had even been told after they were in office, it would have helped us understand what they were doing in spite of the rhetoric which they draped all over it.

44. "For Cheney, Tarnish From Halliburton: Firm's Fall Raises Questions About Vice President's Leadership There," by Dana Milbank, *Washington Post,* Tuesday, July 16, 2002, p. A01.

Knowing the facts and an interpretation of them would have changed the nature of the debate during the 2004 election.

Understanding it now will help us understand what they are doing in their second term.

If we don't like, it will help us find ways to do something about it.

This interpretation of Bushenomics leaves several things unexplained that desperately need explanation.

The president and team are very politically astute people. Why would they pursue these policies if they aren't working now and if they will bring disaster in the future?

If what I am saying is so clear, self-evident, and, more important, true, then why hasn't there been a hue and cry of economists and sociologists and political scientists and babbling heads on *Crossfire* and up and down MSNBC playing the same dolorous chords, sounding the same dire warnings?

Chapter Seven

WHO YOU GONNA BELIEVE, THEM OR YOUR LYING EYES?

JUST AS THERE are Christians there are also Smithians.

A Smithian is someone who believes in the Capitalist Gospels of Adam Smith the Economist as Christians believe in the word of Christ, the Redeemer.

Without a Doubt, by Ron Suskind (*New York Times Magazine,* October 17, 2004), described the role of religious thinking in the White House:

> Faith has . . . shaped [Bush's] presidency in profound, nonreligious ways. The president has demanded unquestioning faith from his followers, his staff, his senior aides and his kindred spirits in the Republican Party. Once he makes a decision—often swiftly, based on a creed or a moral position—he expects complete faith in his rightness. . . .
>
> A writ of infallibility—a premise beneath the powerful Bushian certainty . . . is not just for public

consumption: it has guided the inner life of the White House. As [Christine Todd] Whitman told me on the day in May 2003 that she announced her resignation as administrator of the Environmental Protection Agency, "In meetings I'd ask if there were any facts to support the case. And for that I was accused of disloyalty!"

Whitman later retracted her remarks. Suskind also quotes Bruce Bartlett, a domestic policy adviser to Ronald Reagan and a treasury official under Bush the First, as saying, "I think a light has gone off for people who've spent time up close to Bush: that this instinct he's always talking about is this sort of weird, Messianic idea of what he thinks God has told him to do."

The most significant and striking passage in Suskind's article was this:

I had a meeting with a senior adviser to Bush. He expressed the White House's displeasure, and then he told me something that at the time I didn't fully comprehend—but which I now believe gets to the very heart of the Bush presidency.

The aide said that guys like me were "in what we call the reality-based community," which he defined as people who "believe that solutions emerge from your judicious study of discernible reality." I nodded and murmured something about enlightenment principles and empiricism. He cut me off. "That's not the way the world really works anymore," he continued. "We're an empire now, and when we act, we create our own reality. And while you're studying that reality—judiciously, as

> you will—we'll act again, creating other new realities,
> which you can study too, and that's how things will sort
> out. We're history's actors . . . and you, all of you, will be
> left to just study what we do."

Bush's faith and his "faith-based" choices have been discussed mostly in terms of his crusade-like War on Terror
and the invasions of Afghanistan and Iraq, and in regard to
his social positions. But we instinctively feel that economics
is so intractably by the numbers that it has to be "reality-
based." If you sell pickles at 10 cents apiece, and the operating costs of your pickle stand are $100 a day, and cucumbers
cost 5 cents each, you better sell 2,000 pickles every day just
to break even. You can pray for the price of cukes to fall and
for the craving for marinated vegetables to rise, but faith
wont change a nickel into a dime.

   It's hard to imagine faith-based economics. But that's the
only way that the White House's economic choices and the
administration's commitment to them make sense. As their
religious faith is Christianity—and a near fundamentalist
version of it—their economic faith is Smithianity, and they
treat it like the revealed Word.

   If that's true, we need to know what it is the Smithians
believe, is it reasonable to run a country based on it, and if
it's not, where has the media been?

In 1776 Adam Smith published *The Wealth of Nations*. In it,
he invented modern economics.

   To describe the surprising wonders of what is variously
called free enterprise, free-market capitalism, and laissez-
faire economics, he used the phrase the "invisible hand," thus:

he intends only his own gain, and he is in this, as in many other cases, led by an invisible hand to promote an end which was no part of his intention.

It is typically picked up on in this way:

THE AMAZING INVISIBLE HAND

Smith argued that in a market economy if individuals are allowed to pursue their own self-interests without interference by the government, they would be led, as if by an invisible hand, to achieve what is best for society.

Demystifying Economics: The Book That Makes Economics Accessible to Everyone, Allen W. Smith (Naples, Fla.: P Ironwood Publications, 2000)

This passage is often misquoted as the invisible guiding hand," and "the guiding hand."

With this vivid anthropomorphic phrase, Adam W. Smith also created economic as theology. If an invisible hand is taking the purely self-interested greed of the owner of the strip-mining corporation in West Virginia, and the efforts of Dick Cheney to dump Halliburton's insurance liabilities to people who got lung disease working for the company, and the relentless opposition by Jack Welch's General Electric to cleaning up the Hudson River, and turning them all into what is best for society, that surely must be the Hand of God.

It is natural to think that things need plans. If we are in Chicago and we want to get to Singapore, we do not think that if we just bumble off heading north, something will guide us to an industrious city-state off the tip of Malaysia. If we want to build a railroad, we wouldn't just call a bunch of guys together and say, hey, everybody do your own thing and then line up to get paid at the end of the day. Even this book had a plan at some point.

It was radical and original for Smith to see what was in front of him. That in practice, all these individuals, proceeding each in their own direction for their own purpose, having no regard for anyone else's plan or purpose, somehow were more productive than when King George III's minister of the Exchequer or Louis XVI's minister for finance tried to plan the direction of their nation's economy:

> The natural effort of every individual to better his own condition is so powerful that it is alone, and without any assistance, not only capable of carrying on the society to wealth and prosperity, but of surmounting a hundred impertinent obstructions with which the folly of human laws too often encumbers its operations.

> *The Wealth of Nations,* Adam Smith

The "invisible hand" is a lovely metaphor and a vivid phrase, and as a writer I envy his coining of it. But it is unfortunate because it inevitably suggests something theological. It's not necessary. There are other ways to explain it. For example:

RANDOM STUPIDITY THEORY

Everyone is stupid about something some time.

The most brilliant person in the world will make a

stupid decision occasionally. If that person is in charge of the entire economy, then the whole economy goes in a stupid direction. If that person has stupid subordinates, and they follow his directions stupidly, then the economy will go wrong, too.

In addition, the decision that is correct today will be wrong tomorrow when the environment changes. Knowing when the environment has changed or is about to change is like guessing the stock market. How many people got off the dot.com bubble before it reached its peak and how many stayed in?

The policies that made General Motors the most successful car company in the world are the policies that made it vulnerable to Japanese competition. The polices that took the Japanese economy from a total ruin in 1945 to the envy of the world in the 1980s are the same policies that have had their economy in trouble since the 1990s. Whatever it was that drove Hitler to conquer Western Europe is the same thing that led him to invade Russia and declare war on the United States. The collective genius of IBM said, "We'll do the hardware, you can keep the software, Mr. Gates."

If lots of people are making lots of different choices, some of them are bound to be right sometimes. Many people are still making stupid choices, but when they fail, not everybody fails with them.

When the "invisible hand" is taken literally, the divinity implicit in such a thing turns economics into theology. As is apparent in this article from the Acton Institute for Religion and Liberty.

THE MORAL NATURE OF FREE ENTERPRISE,
THOMAS CARL RUSTICI

The ethical trinity of free enterprise consists of political freedom, individual rights, and private property:

Voluntary cooperation, mutual reciprocity and human respect are [capitalism's] guiding principles.

Force and fraud . . . are inconsistent with free enterprise. Contracts are based upon respect for the property rights of others. Bargaining replaces violence and domination in moral and legal disputes. Honesty and integrity uphold the spirit of contract as well as reinforce human character. Prosperity and social harmony naturally flow from the ethical virtues of free enterprise.

[Capitalism] directs unbridled human greed into socially beneficial outcomes. The market, then, becomes a win-win process, not a "zero-sum game" where the victors plunder the losers in their acquisition of wealth. Both parties to the transaction must gain, or voluntary social cooperation ends.

Capitalism demolishes all economic barriers unleashing our maximum human potential.

[Capitalism] also produces international peace. . . . People preoccupied with earning money have little time to engage in warfare.

Or this, from the *National Review* Online (February 18, 2004)

"WEALTH AND VIRTUE:
THE MORAL CASE FOR CAPITALISM"
MICHAEL NOVAK (AUTHOR, PHILOSOPHER, THEOLOGIAN)

1. . . . break the habit of servile dependency . . .
2. . . . awaken the poor from isolation and indolence,
3. . . . diminish warlikeness . . .
4. . . . bring the peoples of each country into closer, more frequent, and complex interaction.
5. . . . break down class barriers, stimulate upward mobility, encourage literacy and civil discourse,
6. . . . augment "human capital" . . . new specialties, skills, and techniques . . .
7. . . . teach the necessity of civility . . .
8. . . . soften manners . . . develop the high moral art of sympathy.
9. . . . train citizens in the arts of being farsighted, objective, and future-oriented. . . . Such public-spiritedness is a virtue that is good, not merely because it is useful, but because it seeks to be in line, in however humble a way, with the future common good.
10. . . . defeat envy . . . A capitalist system defeats envy, and promotes in its place the personal pursuit of happiness. It does this by generating invention, discovery, and economic growth. Its ideal is win-win, a situation in which everyone wins.

There is no doubt whatsoever that there is lots of truth in all of that. Personally, I like capitalism, I like money, I like the creativity and products that they bring. I like freedom. I've run a business and thought it was pretty great. But I didn't like certain aspects of it, like selling and bookkeeping and getting along with others, so I went into another business that seemed to require much less of that, writing, and more of what I like, which is making things.

But that does not mean that capitalism and capitalists are without flaws.

Indeed, the history of capitalism, in addition to booms and productivity and creativity, is one of crashes, panics, busts, ruin, exploitation, looting, fraud, violence, murder, imperialism, wars, waste, and the despoliation of the land. Left to its own devices, it destroys individuals, communities, and cultures and it will even destroy itself. It seemed about to do so with the Crash of 1929 and the Great Depression of the 1930s:

> One out of every four American workers lacked a job. Hunger marchers, pinched and bitter, were parading cold streets in New York and Chicago.
>
> *Crises of the Old Order,* Arthur M. Schlesinger Jr.

Not only had capitalism failed, but the capitalist democracies seemed unable to do anything about it. In Germany, unemployment went from 650,000 in 1928 to 6,100,000 in 1933. In England, unemployment doubled in 1930. In some of the cities of the industrial north of England, unemployment reached 70 percent.

By 1929 there were newer economic and political models to choose from.

Communism had arisen as a theory in response to the excesses and brutalities of capitalism in the mid-nineteenth century.

In 1917, Russia became a communist country.

Fascism arose as an alternative to both free-market capitalism and parliamentary democracy. Hungary became the first fascist state in 1919. Italy became fascist in 1922. In 1932, Hitler came to power in Germany.

In 1933 Franklin Roosevelt became president of the United States and began the New Deal, which can be described as democracy and capitalism with government tinkering.

It introduced regulations to banking and to the stock market. It created Social Security and unemployment insurance. It tried a variety of public works programs with varying degrees of success. It raised taxes on the wealthy.

There is a great deal of argument over how effective all of this was and whether the New Deal got America out of the Depression or whether the country just wobbled along until the war came and wartime spending made the difference. Whichever it was, America's gross domestic product increased 90 percent from the time Roosevelt took office in 1933 to the time we entered the war in 1941. America did not go either fascist or communist. It did, however, empower a lot people who had no power before:

> As a result of the New Deal, U.S. political and economic life became much more competitive than before, with workers, farmers, consumers, and others now able to press their demands upon the government in ways that in the past had been available only to the corporate world.

Wikipedia, the Free Encyclopedia online

That all sounds fine to me. And, indeed, to the average American it's been fine for the last seventy-five years.

A Smithian fundamentalist believes that a completely free market will work things out for the best. For everyone. Any pain and confusion along the war are salutary; they are "market discipline." All taxes and all regulations are bad, because they restrict the market. The government is the enemy because the government taxes and regulates. Social services are downright evil:

FREEDOM VERSUS THE WELFARE STATE

> The problem with the welfare state is that it is immoral in principle and disastrous in practice. It sets citizen against citizen, and undermines families and communities, discourages self-responsibility and civic action, slows economic growth and locks the most vulnerable into poverty.

> Doug Bandow, senior fellow at the Cato Institute[45]

Walter E. Williams, the John M. Olin Distinguished Professor of Economics at George Mason University and a senior fellow at both the Heritage Foundation and the Hoover Institution, bases all morality on property rights and then equates taxation with rape:

> Once one accepts the principle of self-ownership, what's moral and immoral becomes self-evident. Murder is immoral because it violates private property. Rape and theft are also immoral—they also violate private property.

45. www.cato.org/dailys/2-12-97.html.

Here's an important question: Would rape become morally acceptable if Congress passed a law legalizing it? You say: "What's wrong with you, Williams? Rape is immoral plain and simple, no matter what Congress says or does!"

If you take that position, isn't it just as immoral when Congress legalizes the taking of one person's earnings to give to another?[46]

To the Smithian, socialism, Bolshevism and communism are the forces of Satan. They see Roosevelt as Darwin and the New Deal as evolution. It shows that capitalism can be tinkered with by man, and if it can be tinkered with by man, it is not divine, and if it is not divine . . . why then, what is to stop us from embracing the sloth of socialism and utter debasement of Marxist-Leninism. *Godless* communism.

The Bush administration is not intent on destroying Social Security because it doesn't work or because it won't work sometime in the future. They're going after it because it does work and it represents the success of a heretical sect:

Social Security is the soft underbelly of the welfare state. If you can jab your spear through that, you can undermine the whole welfare state.

Stephen Moore, senior fellow, Cato Institute, contributing editor, *National Review,* president of the Free Enterprise Fund

By which he means: if the most cherished and popular program can be killed, the rest will fall.

46. www.townhall.com/columnists/walterwilliams/ww20030507.shtml.

Chapter Eight

STEALING IN PLAIN SIGHT

I HAVE, THROUGHOUT this book, cited news stories as my sources. Clearly, I believe that if something has been in the *Washington Post,* CNN, NBC News, CBS News, and a host of other publications, it is a certified fact.

Obviously, there have been exceptions and mistakes in all these outlets. But they are fairly rare. They are usually examined if challenged, and corrected if demonstrated to be false. Our journalism professionals have standards and they endeavor to maintain them.[47]

47. In May 2005, *Newsweek* printed a story that an upcoming Pentagon investigation would say that U.S. government interrogators had tried to flush a Koran down the toilet. *Newsweek* had shown the article to two Pentagon spokespersons before it was printed. Neither one denied it. Eleven days after the story was published, the Pentagon said it was not true that such an incident was in the report. *Newsweek* retracted the specific statement that the allegation was in a Pentagon report in a matter of days. The rest of the media treated the retraction as if they had retracted the story or the allegation.

The White House made as much of the incident as it could. An anonymous source, described by the *New York Times* (May 18, 2005) as a "Bush advisor" explained why: "In the course of any administration you have three

As for the *New York Times*, I hold it in almost as high esteem as it holds itself. It is the paper I cite the most often because it is what I read by choice and because it is close to being what it intends to be: the newspaper of record.

David Brock, the author of *Blinded by the Right: Conscience of an Ex-Conservative,* says in his new book, *The Republican Noise Machine:*

> People ask me, a former insider, how the Republican Right has won political and ideological power with such seeming ease and why Democrats seem to be . . . steadily losing the battle for hearts and minds. . . . My answer is: It's the media, stupid.

Both are true. The mainstream media maintains standards and the mainstream media is a big part of the problem.

Here's my favorite news story about postwar Iraq.

It is from the *New York Times*, June 21, 2004. The writer is Steven R. Weisman, the *Times*'s chief diplomatic correspondent, based in Washington, D.C.

U.S. IS QUIETLY SPENDING $2.5 BILLION FROM IRAQI
OIL REVENUES TO PAY FOR IRAQI PROJECTS

> Struggling with bureaucratic problems in spending the money appropriated by Congress to rebuild Iraq, American authorities are moving quietly and quickly to

---

or four opportunities, at most, with a high-profile press mistake."

I cite that as an estimate of how rare such errors are.

It is worth noting that about two weeks afterward, the allegation showed up in an FBI report.

spend $2.5 billion from a different source, Iraqi oil revenue, for projects employing tens of thousands of Iraqis, especially in the country's hot spots, Bush administration officials say.

The spending program, which was started unannounced, has been undertaken in consultation with Iraqi ministers, despite misgivings that the oil revenue belonged to Iraq and that it should be set aside for use when Iraq's sovereignty is restored, scheduled for June 30.

Because of deteriorating security and complex delays in contracts that have slowed the spending of the $18 billion in Congressionally appropriated money, occupation authorities say they decided recently that they had to spend the Iraqi money to build schools, factories and oil fields, and to turn Iraqis away from violence.

"The security needs were just overwhelming," said an occupation official. "Would we rather have been able to save the money and have a nice kitty? Sure. There's always a tension between putting money to work right away and having it available for a tough year next year. This is the way we resolved it." . . .

[It] helped pay for security needs like police cars and uniforms, as well as repairs of schools, power grids, oil fields, state-owned factories and other sources of employment . . . for vocational training for young Iraqis "to get some of these kids off the streets, doing something productive for the future," an occupation official said. . . .

[It was] spent on 15 to 21 military or security projects around the country . . . for vocational training, infrastructure repair . . . and increased supplies of food.

A principal goal is to employ Iraqis. . . .

One reason for distributing cash for quick gains,

some administration officials say, is that controls on the $18 billion appropriated by Congress last fall to rebuild Iraq may make it harder to operate in that fashion, so policy makers have decided to use what they have before the formal end of the occupation, now scheduled for June 30.

Of the $18 billion appropriated by Congress, . . . only $3.2 billion in contracts for actual construction projects have been awarded. . . .

Occupation officials say the spending of money now to generate employment will revive state industries. . . .

"There are two ways of looking at this," the official said. "First is the absolute need to find jobs for millions of young people who need training. But second is to increase the capacity of companies and of the oil infrastructure to become healthy and employ more Iraqis in the future."

It sounds as if some imaginative and caring occupation officials faced with urgent problems overcame that typical "cumbersome," "complex," bureaucratic red tape, rolled up their sleeves, and got the job done. They didn't even slow down to hold a press conference. Because the Iraqi people needed jobs. In the full story, the word "jobs" is used three times, "training" is used three times, and "employment" or "employing" is used nine times. And it's about "security." The need for security made them do it, the problems with security kept them from doing something else, and what they're doing will provide security.

But if you strip the "explanations" out of the story, you get this:

The United States Congress appropriated over $18 billion dollars for the reconstruction of Iraq. That money was not being used. One reason was the controls on how the money was to be spent. The story does not specify what those controls were. The story also refers to security issues. But the security issues were the same no matter where the money came from.

There was another pile of money. It was being held in trust for Iraq. It was supposed to be handed over when an Iraqi government was in place, so that they could spend their own money.

Instead of spending the money that was appropriated for the job, unnamed American officials, from an unnamed organization, decided to spend the money that was being held in trust. Precisely because it did not have controls on it.

They deliberately did not tell anyone.

The date for the transfer of power, when the money would have to be handed over, had just been moved up. So the Americans were rushing to spend the money faster, before that transfer took place.

The most wonderful bit is in the middle of the story:

Some of the money has gone to American military teams operating since the beginning of the occupation 14 months ago. The teams have become famous in Iraq for the way they have spread across the country, commissioning repairs and paying for them from satchels bulging with $100 bills shipped by plane from a Federal Reserve vault in East Rutherford, N.J. Much of that money came from Iraqi assets frozen in the United States during the Persian Gulf war in 1991.

This is not a movie. This is real life.

Planeloads of $100 bills were being flown from a vault in New Jersey to Iraq. In Iraq they are being given to army guys. Regular army guys. In suitcases. Who go and do stuff with it. There are no records. No accounts. Nor is there anywhere in this story, or elsewhere that I have found, a list of wells dug, sewers repaired, schools built, books bought and distributed, health clinics established. One thing we know about this administration: if there were good works done, they would have had embedded journalists there in bed with them, or they would have made their own video news releases with people who play reporters on TV, and we would have seen it.

You may wonder how much money was distributed in this fashion:

> At least $1 billion has been distributed in this fashion— by some estimates more than $2 billion.
> "The military commanders love that program, . . ." said an administration official.

Yeah, I bet they do.

Let us assume that there are guys in the Army you can give suitcases full of cash to, who know that it will never have to be accounted for, who will not put it somewhere safe to provide for their family's future, and who will actually spend it on Iraqi reconstruction projects. Still, imagine how much fun it must be, running around Iraq, in your Humvee, handing out wads of Benjamins like a coke dealer on *Miami Vice*.

I spoke with Steve Weisman, the author of the article above. He did not feel that the story was full of spin. His feeling is that "quietly," did not convey the modesty of a shy philanthropist but did suggest secretive practices. I said the facts suggested opportunities for embezzlement and out-right theft. He said there was no evidence that would allow the story to go there. Unless someone had been charged or arrested, then it was unsayable, almost unthinkable. He also expressed that he thought there was more there and would have liked to have pushed the story further, but his editors were not interested.

Actually, the $2.5 billion was just the tip of the iceberg.

Iraq surrendered at the end of March 2003. Paul Bremer III took charge of the CPA at the beginning of April. CPA stands for Coalition Provisional Authority, not Certified Public Accountant.

The CPA took charge of Iraq's money. There has been no formal statement or accounting of how much that was. A best guess by Christian Aid, a major British charitable organization, is that there was $2.5 billion in seized funds in bank accounts around the world and $1 billion in the United Nations Oil for Food Program when the CPA took over. The CPA also began collecting Iraq's oil revenues. Presumably on behalf of Iraq.

In October, 2003 there was a conference in Madrid at which the United States asked other governments how much they would be willing to give toward Iraqi reconstruction.

Christian Aid could not find out how much money the CPA had or how it was being spent. They estimated that by then there was $9 billion under CPA control, the additional sums coming from oil revenue, plus more money from the Oil for Food Program. They prepared a report that they presented to the Madrid conference and to the media. It said:

> *. . . incredibly, these billions of dollars of Iraqi oil rev-*
> *enues have never been publicly accounted for.* Christian
> Aid has discovered a black hole into which these funds
> have disappeared. The black hole is presided over not
> by an Iraqi government, but by the CPA, the de facto
> ruling authority established by the forces occupying
> Iraq. The US dominates the CPA.[48]

That cry of outrage was not noticed in the United States. It
brought about no change.

The first media story about the missing billions that I
could find was in May 2004. Andrew Cockburn did a story
in Salon: "Raiding Iraq's Piggy Bank." Iraqi oil sales for 2004
were expected to be over $16 billion. Due to UN Security
Resolution 1483, control of the money went to the occupying
power. Which was the United States as the CPA, which put
the money into the DFI, Development Fund for Iraq, which
had only one Iraqi member. By then, oil-for-food transfers
into the fund were up to $8.1 billion, and there was $1.3
billion in cash found in Iraq.

By then, DFI had given out about $7.3 billion. But
nobody knew to whom or for what.

Cockburn explained what it actually was that the *New
York Times* had called "bureaucratic problems in spending
the money appropriated by Congress to rebuild Iraq" and
the "complex delays in contracts." After the Halliburton
scandals in 2003, Congress passed a law requiring competi-
tive bids on any contract worth over $5 million.

48. "Iraq: The Missing Billions: Transition and Transparency in Post-War
Iraq," briefing paper for the Madrid conference on Iraq, 23–24 October,
2003, Christian Aid, available at www.christianaid.org.uk/indepth/
310iraqoil/index.htm.

In October 2003, Bush asked Congress for an $87-billion dollar supplemental spending bill. It was universally referred to as the Iraq Reconstruction Bill. But $69 billion was for military operations and only $18 billion was for reconstruction. This was on top of over $3 billion previously set aside for reconstruction.

Of that $21 billion, only $10.5 billion was actually spent on reconstruction while the CPA was running the country.

But by July, a month after the *New York Times* story, it was apparent that almost all the money that belonged to the Iraqis was gone:

> U.S. officials in charge of the Development Fund for Iraq drained all but $900 million from the $20 billion fund by late last month in what a watchdog group has called an "11th hour splurge."

> Mark Matthews, *Baltimore Sun,* July 3, 2004

But where? Where did the money go? Here's one perfect tidbit:

> One chunk of the money—$1.4 billion—was deposited into a local bank by Kurdish leaders in northern Iraq but could be tracked no further. The auditors reported that they were shown a deposit slip but could find no additional record to explain how the money was used or to prove that it remains in the bank.

> Bryan Bender, *Boston Globe,* October 16, 2004

The CPA has been dissolved. It is now impossible to do a real audit. Should Iraq someday become a real nation, wonder where their money went, and try to go after it or the people who handed out approximately $19 billion dollars with virtually nothing to show for it, they will not be able to. Even if it turns out that the money was put right in someone's pocket, not just badly handled. On May 22, 2003, ten days after Paul Bremer arrived in Iraq to run the CPA, George W. Bush issued Executive Order 13303:

> The threat of attachment or judicial process against the Development Fund for Iraq, Iraqi petroleum and petroleum products, and interests therein . . . constitutes an unusual and extraordinary threat to the national security and foreign policy of the United States. . . . Any . . . judicial process is prohibited, and shall be deemed null and void.

Once again, a class of people has deemed itself above the law.

This, to my mind, is a great story. Nineteen billion dollars in cash disappeared. It makes the best and the biggest mafia heist small time. It's got guys filling up bags with Benjamins and throwing them in the backs of pick-up trucks. It's got a race to hand out ten billion dollars in a matter of months. It's an entire country ripped off. It's the story of a vital job not done. A country left without water, sewers, schools, and security. And the man in charge, L. Paul Bremer, gets the Presidential Medal of Freedom.

STATEMENT ON PRESIDENTIAL MEDAL OF FREEDOM RECIPIENTS

STATEMENT BY THE PRESS SECRETARY

President Bush will award the Presidential Medal of Freedom to L. Paul Bremer III, Tommy R. Franks, and George J. Tenet in a ceremony at the White House on December 14, 2004.

The Presidential Medal of Freedom is the Nation's highest civil award. It was established by President Truman and later re-established by President Kennedy. It is awarded by the President of the United States to persons who have made especially meritorious contributions to the security or national interests of the United States, to world peace, or to cultural or other significant public or private endeavors.

Chapter Nine

THE SOFT MACHINE

NOBODY SUPPRESSED THE STORIES about the looting of Iraq.

When they were published, nobody censored them.

When I spoke with Steve Brill and when I spoke with Clarence Page, a syndicated *Chicago Tribune* columnist, when I was fortunate enough to spend a day with the news team of *NBC Nightly News*, everybody spoke about the media's story selections in terms of the same thing, a combination of their duty to report the news and market forces.

That's why you know more about Terry Schiavo's husband, brother, mother, and father than you do about the looting of Iraq.

The election of 2000 was stolen. Twice.

Those were quintessential fog facts, at least through 2003. Knowable, but unknown. Discoverable, but only if you first knew to look.

The first theft was accomplished before the election. Greg

Palast discovered that the state of Florida had managed to dis-
enfranchise tens of thousands of African-American voters.

BLACK-OUT IN FLORIDA

> Vice President Al Gore would have strolled to victory
> in Florida if the state hadn't kicked up to 66,000 citizens
> off the voter registers five months ago as former felons.
> In fact, not all were ex-cons. Most were simply guilty of
> being African-American.

> *The Observer,* London, November 26, 2000

That story was printed while the recount was still going on.

No media outlet in the United States would take the
story. It was only printed and broadcast in Europe.

If that had been printed in the *New York Times* or the
Washington Post on CNN or CBS, would the Supreme
Court still have dared to stop the recount?

Long after the election, the U.S. Civil Rights Commission held hearings about the disenfranchisement of
voters. Their draft report, *Voting Irregularities in Florida
During the 2000 Presidential Election* published June 8,
2001, stated:

- Black voters were nearly 10 times more likely than non-
  black voters to have their ballots rejected. Poor counties, particularly those with large minority populations,
  were more likely to possess voting systems with higher
  spoilage rates than the more affluent counties with significant white populations. There is a high correlation
  between counties and precincts with a high percentage

of African American voters and the percentage of spoiled ballots, that is, ballots cast but not counted.

- Nine of the 10 counties with the highest percentage of African American voters had spoilage rates above the Florida average.
- Of the 10 counties with the highest percentage of white voters, only two counties had spoilage rates above the state average.
- Gadsden County, with the highest rate of spoiled ballots, also had the highest percentage of African American voters.
- Where precinct data were available, the data show that 83 of the 100 precincts with the highest numbers of disqualified ballots are black-majority precincts.[49]

Florida's optical-scan voting machines could be set two ways. They could throw away ballots that were not correctly marked or they could return them to the voters to be corrected. The machines in counties with large black and poor populations were set to eat bad ballots. The machines in whiter and more prosperous counties were set to politely return improperly marked ballots to be corrected. That's what being white and middle-class is all about.

Palast asked the clerk who showed him the machines if the people who maintained them and preset them before they were sent to different counties were aware of the racial profiles of the counties where the different machines went.

"We've been waiting for someone to ask us that." The clerk then pulled out a huge multicolored sheet, listing, for

49. permanent.access.gpo.gov/lps13588/lps13588/exsum.htm.

every Florida county, the number of ballots not counted. The proportion of uncounted ballots to the Black population, county by county, was a nearly perfect match. . . .

Then I got the 64 Dollar questions: What did [Katherine] Harris and the governor [Jeb Bush] know and when did they know it. . . . The technicians told me, "That's why we set up this machine, so they could see it—*before* the election."[50]

The *Wall Street Journal* (October 12, 2001) also noted the discrepancies: "While Florida's overall rejection rate was just under 3%, the rate was nearly four times as high in precincts that are predominantly black."

But the authors, Jackie Calmes and Edward P. Foldessy, were able to find a very delicate way of blaming it on the po' ignorant black folk:

Thousands more Gore voters than Bush voters appear to have been foiled by a combination of their own mistakes and confusing ballots . . . such overvotes tended to be more frequent in counties with more black voters and lower-income voters—suggesting that many resulted from a combination of poor ballot design, less education and less experience in voting.

A May 2005 Google search for the phrase "Florida election 2000 stolen" did not turn up a single story from a mainstream American media source. It was as if the word "stolen" could not even be printed in the same sentence with the words "election, Florida," and "2000."

50. Palast, *Best Democracy Money Can Buy,* p. 64.

A Lexis-Nexis search brought up two references. The *San Francisco Chronicle* ran a story on January 1, 2001, about protesters who were saying the election was stolen, and the *Boston Globe* on November 23, 2000, had this:

> Republicans counter that if Gore ends up eking out a victory, he will be viewed by many as having stolen the election. Worse, some Republicans said, Gore will have done it on the backs of some military personnel whose votes had been disqualified.

On election day George Bush appeared to have taken Florida by a few hundred votes. The law in Florida was actually quite simple and direct:

> If the returns for any office reflect that a candidate was defeated or eliminated by one-half of a percent or less of the votes cast for such office, . . . the board responsible for certifying the results of the vote on such race or measure shall order a recount of the votes cast with respect to such office or measure.

That is one of the most clearly written bits of legislation I've ever seen anywhere.

The Florida court thought so, too, and ordered a recount.

Then the legal maneuvering began. There were local suits and federal suits and state pleadings. Then the United States Supreme Court stepped in and shut the recounts down. None of the many possible recounts ever took place.

Bush was left as the victor and became the president.

But presumably the whole world wanted to know who

actually did get the most votes. It would make a great and important story. The *New York Times*, the *Washington Post*, the Tribune Company, the *Wall Street Journal*, the Associated Press, the *Los Angeles Times*, the *St. Petersburg Times*, the *Palm Beach Post*, and CNN formed a consortium to share the expense of counting the votes and finding out the truth.

It took almost a year and cost over a million dollars. And here are the headlines:

> *New York Times*: "Study of Disputed Florida Ballots Finds Justices Did Not Cast the Deciding Vote"
> *Wall Street Journal:* "In Election Review, Bush Wins Without Supreme Court Help"
> *Los Angeles Times:* "Bush Still Had Votes to Win in a Recount, Study Finds"
> *Washington Post:* "Florida Recounts Would Have Favored Bush"
> CNN.com: "Florida Recount Study: Bush Still Wins"
> *St. Petersburg Times:* "Recount: Bush"

That's very clear.

If you went past the headlines and read the stories, it would, in most cases, only reinforce the impression.

I read it in the *New York Times*. Now, having gone back and read them all, I've discovered that the *Times* was the worst of the lot. They spent the first three paragraphs supporting the headline and they explicitly stated that Bush would have won even with a statewide recount.

Finally, in the fourth paragraph—if you got that far—was this statement:

If all the ballots had been reviewed under any of seven single standards, and combined with the results of an examination of overvotes, Mr. Gore would have won, by a very narrow margin.

There it is. A very simple statement. Al Gore got more votes in Florida than George Bush.

It is also very well buried. It's got arcania about chads on both sides of it. When I read the story at the time it was published, I didn't notice it at all.

Even so, as if in a panic to make sure that nobody might think that it mattered that Al Gore got more votes than George Bush, the *Times* dismissed what the consortium had spent a million dollars to find out:

While these are fascinating findings, they do not represent a real-world situation. There was no set of circumstances in the fevered days after the election that would have produced a hand recount of all 175,000 overvotes and undervotes.

Even though that would seem to be a fairly obvious interpretation of the law and it is what was found when someone actually did sit down and count the votes.

The rest of the story, another four paragraphs, details a variety of other possible recounts, all partial recounts— these counties, but not those counties—that the Gore lawyers or the Bush lawyers asked for at various times. Bush would have won all of those variations; he just didn't get the most votes in Florida.

Technicalities: Undervotes and Overvotes

An undervote is a vote that the voting machine cannot read. If it's the punch system, the "chad" would not have been completely punched through.

An overvote is when a voter checked Al Gore's name and then wrote "Al Gore" on the ballot as well. The machine does not reason, it simply rejects that as too many marks.

The Florida court originally called for a count of the undervotes.

If only the undervotes are counted, Bush wins.

The people doing the private recount noticed the overvotes. They counted them too. If the undervotes and the overvotes are counted, Gore wins.

This technicality allowed the various media outlets to say that Bush would have won the recount and to make the other very important claim that the Supreme Court's intervention would not have changed the outcome.

That's important because the five justices who voted to stop the recount clearly voted against their own records and judicial philosophies. If their action didn't matter, then their betrayal of judicial duty didn't matter. At least not that much.

I spoke to a reporter who had worked on the *Miami Herald* recount which had taken place and been published six months earlier. For them, the whole issue was whether the Supreme Court's decision had made the difference.[51] Since it hadn't, he regarded it all as settled.

What if, I asked him, the folks doing a real recount had

51. *The Miami Herald Report: Democracy Held Hostage,* Martin Merzer and the Staff of the Pulitzer Prize-Winning *Miami Herald*, (St. Martin's Press, May 2001.)

come across the same thing you guys did, that there were overvotes not counted, and they had gone to the court and said: Here are these other kinds of votes, they weren't counted, but we can determine clearly the intent of the voter, which is the Florida standard—shouldn't we count them too?

The idea had apparently never occurred to any of the reporters or editors. After our conversation I looked, and lo and behold, that was exactly what had been happening:

> *Newsweek* has uncovered hastily scribbled faxed notes written by Terry Lewis, the plain-speaking, mystery-novel writing state judge in charge of the Florida recount. . . . Just hours before the U.S. Supreme Court issued its order [to halt the recount]—Lewis was actively considering directing the counties to also count an even larger category of disputed ballots, the so-called "overvotes," which were rejected by the machines because they purportedly recorded more than one vote for president. . . . "Judge, if you would, segregate 'over-votes' as you describe and indicate in your final report how many where you determined the clear intent of the voter," Lewis wrote in a note to Judge W. Wayne Woodard, chairman of the Charlotte County Can-vassing Board on the afternoon of December 9, 2000. "I will rule on the issue for all counties, Thanks, Terry Lewis."
>
> *Newsweek*, "The Final Word?" Michael Isikoff,
> November 19, 2001

Brent Cunningham, the managing editor of the *Columbia*

Journalism Review, expressed the emotional code of the journalist as follows:

> The bias, ultimately, was toward the story. . . . We are biased in favor of getting the story, regardless of whose ox is being gored. Listen to Daniel Bice, an investigative columnist at the *Milwaukee Journal-Sentinel*, summarize his reporting philosophy: "Try not to be boring, be a reliable source of information, cut through the political, corporate, and bureaucratic bullshit, avoid partisanship, and hold politicians' feet to the fire." It would be tough to find a reporter who disagrees with any of that. . . .
>
> Reporters are biased toward conflict because it is more interesting than stories without conflict.

The consumer's assumption, and the promise of the invisible hand, is that if there is a good story, and if somebody tries to suppress it, then somebody else will publish or broadcast it, because they will make more money or get better ratings. The pursuit of profits will keep the media honest and ensure that the truth will out!

Here are two possible stories: ELECTION STOLEN! or NO SURPRISE, BUSH ACTUALLY WON.

"Election Stolen" is, hands down, the exciting one. The grabber. The conflict. The drama. For God's sakes, Bush won is *olds,* only "Election Stolen" is *news.*

Why did all the media decide to run with the dull, with the boring, with the *olds?*

It's easy to understand why in an immediate way. The election recount stories are dated November 12, 2001, just thirty-one days after September 11th. It was not the time to announce that president of the United States was illegitimate.

How this happened is more problematic. Did a senior editor sit down in a conference with the reporter and the editor and the headline writer and tell them: You can put the truth in, but you have to bury it so nobody will notice?

Even more intriguing is the question of how all these incredibly prestigious, independent, and presumably competing media enterprises decided to participate in the same deception? They're all in the business of selling the same things: integrity and truth, accurate information that we can count on. How did they all come to lie—at the very least mislead—all with one voice.

It seems unlikely that Arthur Ochs Sulzburger, the publisher of the *New York Times*, had a conference call with his opposite numbers at the *Washington Post*, the *Wall Street Journal*, CNN, and CBS to say: All right, guys, this is how we're running this one.

Something else happened.

Call it the Soft Machine.

In the eighteenth century the culture of independent artisans and small entrepreneurs was a refreshing opposition to a jaded aristocracy and to countries run by sycophantic ministers to decadent monarchs, and the idea of an invisible hand was roughly true.

But capitalism has matured. Like all systems, its first duty is to itself. The Soft Machine is its security system, its enforcement arm and its army of conquest. Like the Internet, it is a work of unconsciously cooperative genius. Where the invisible hand guided all the individual greedy efforts into a greater good, the Soft Machine guides all individual efforts either into atrophy or into the greater good of the capitalist system.

Noam Chomsky is right. Consent is manufactured in modern capitalist democracies. Frequently there is little more significant dissent in democracies than in totalitarian systems. The qualifiers *"frequently," "significant," and "little more"* are very significant. Soft-Machine states are vastly more comfortable places to live in—and especially to dissent in—than totalitarian states are.

Totalitarian societies use the Hard Machine. They are called police states. All those policeman are expensive. Police are necessary, but the more order you can have without police, the more efficient the society is. Just as the conquest of foreign states by business is more economical than conquest by force of arms. Conquest by business makes money. Conquest by force of arms always costs money.

Furthermore, the dysfunction of a police state is greater than merely the cost of the salaries and equipment of the constabulary. Police states are command societies. No matter how brilliant the people at the top are, random stupidity always kicks in. The harder the machine, the more certain it becomes that bad decisions will be enforced and remain in force.

Inherent rigidity and its maintenance of stupidity are the primary reason for the collapse of the Soviet Union.

The genius of the Soft Machine is the genius of capitalism. It accepts a certain amount of anarchy. It sorts out and controls multiple voices with money. Multiple voices are important because the quality of being right is, to a certain degree, random. At a given time, it comes from logic, at another, from intuition. It might come from faith, from dreaming, from inspiration, and sometimes just from luck.

The Soft Machine can absorb conflicting ideas. While

lots of people in the West regard our environmental record as dreadful, it is far superior to what happened in the old East Bloc, where the commissars simply ordered the rivers to be dammed, the lakes to be drained, and the nuclear waste to be dumped.

The Soft Machine will readily absorb radical ideas, too, so long as they are moneymakers, and it will turn them into profits or souvenirs. The sexual revolution has become the multibillion-dollar porn industry. Rap is now all *bling-bling*. Bohemian styles have been the mainstay of chain stores in the mall since the birth of the mall. Che is a road movie and a T-shirt too. Malcolm X is a stamp.

Do you fear the Soft Machine or desire its embrace? If you have an idea, a great idea, an idea that people want, an idea that stirs things up and changes things, the Soft Machine will pay you for it. It will make it a product and bring it to market. Make you rich and famous and treat you with great, if temporary, respect.

The Soft Machine has, and will use, the hard instruments of power and rule. The Soft Machine does not give up police and military powers. Indeed, the United States is the world leader in the number of people imprisoned, in the employment of military force, in the possession and use of weapons of mass destruction. But we use those hard instruments only in the context of a consensus, however that consensus is built or has come about.

The Hard Machine uses the hard powers of a police state to suppress dissent and force that consensus. The mechanisms of control are visible: midnight arrests, the secret police, the informers, the political prisons, the disappeared people.

By contrast, you almost never see the Soft Machine as it moves to herd us all together. Sometimes, as with the misreporting of the election results, although you can't see it, you can see that something must have happened.

The Soft Machine is hard to fight.

Whom or what do you punch? It's not punching you. It's just offering you something to buy, and it's your choice to buy a fatten-you-up burger, and to wear cheap, slave-labor jeans from Wal-Mart. No one forces you to get your news from Fox and to zone out on reality shows.

The Soft Machine not only manufactures consent, it convinces you that it's doing it as a favor to you. You are a consumer and it is your choice of consumptions that dictates to the manufacturer what to make. Since the process is serving you, that puts you, de facto, in charge of that process. Fox News—and the *New York Times*—say what they say because it's what you want to hear.

As to limiting debate, well, that's up to you, too. The truths about the 2000 election, for example—both the disenfranchisement of African-American voters and that the recount would have favored Gore—were available. Obscurely and marginally. But available. And if enough people had gotten excited about them and flocked to them, then they would have become part of the debate. The proof is that in 2004 both issues did become part of the national noise.

You can't fight the Soft Machine. You don't want to. The Soft Machine is you.

Chapter Ten

THE LAND OF INVISIBLE CORPSES

―――――――――

[t]he humanity that goes into it.

Donald Rumsfeld

SHOCK AND AWE

In March 2003, the United States invaded Iraq.

There was a brief attempt to "get" Saddam Hussein just before the main operations commenced. Then came Shock and Awe.

Shock and Awe was an event, a theory, and a demonstration. The event was a huge bombardment conducted almost entirely by the United States. It consisted of approximately 14,000 sorties using a variety of fighters and bombers. They fired cannons, shot missiles, and dropped bombs. An additional 800 land and sea-based missiles were part of the attack.

All of this explosive power was directed primarily at Baghdad, a city of 5,800,000 people, Mosul, with 1,770,000 people, and the town of Tikrit, with about 28,000 people.

The theory was that if sufficiently shocked, an enemy would be so awestruck that it wouldn't know what to do and would simply surrender in abject terror. The outlines of the strategy were laid out in *Shock and Awe: Achieving Rapid Dominance,* published by the press arm of the National Defense University:[52]

> Theoretically, the magnitude Shock and Awe Rapid Dominance seeks to impose (in extreme cases) is the non-nuclear equivalent of the impact that the atomic weapons dropped on Hiroshima and Nagasaki had on the Japanese. The Japanese were prepared for suicidal resistance until both nuclear bombs were used. The impact of those weapons was sufficient to transform both the mindset of the average Japanese citizen and the outlook of the leadership through this condition of Shock and Awe. The Japanese simply could not comprehend the destructive power carried by a single airplane. This incomprehension produced a state of awe.
>
> We believe that, in a parallel manner, revolutionary potential in combining new doctrine and existing technology can produce systems capable of yielding this level of Shock and Awe. In most or many cases, this Shock and Awe may not necessitate imposing the full

52. Harlan K. Ullman and James P. Wade with L.A. "Bud" Edney, Fred M. Franks, Charles A. Horner, Jonathan T. Howe, and Keith Brendley (Washington, D.C.: NDU Press, 1966), available online at www.ndu.edu /inss/books/books%20-%201996/Shock%20and%20Awe%20%20Dec%2096/ index.html.

destruction of either nuclear weapons or advanced conventional technologies but must be underwritten by the ability to do so.

It was a live event shown to the world on international television. It was visually impressive, a giant fireworks show with special effects and special night-viewing devices. Great explosions, gouts of flame, plumes of smoke, and the very earth was seen to tremble.

The intent was not just to shock and awe Iraq but to shock and awe the entire world with a display of unmatchable American might. Its designers hoped it would turn out to be the most influential display of unchallengeable power since Hiroshima and Nagasaki.

It was also presented to the world as a humanitarian means of warfare. The shock would create instant surrender and there wouldn't even have to be a war. Also, the missiles and bombs that delivered the shock would only hit military targets. On March 21, 2003, Donald Rumsfeld told Jim Lehrer:

Just before coming down, after the air campaign began in earnest about one, I saw some of the images on television and I heard various commentators expansively comparing what's taking place in Iraq today to some of the more famous bombing campaigns of World War II. There is no comparison. The weapons that are being used today have a degree of precision that no one ever dreamt of in a prior conflict: They didn't exist. And it's not a handful of weapons, it's the overwhelming majority of the weapons that have that precision. *The targeting capabilities and the*

*care that goes into targeting to see that the precise targets
are struck and that other targets are not struck, is as
impressive as anything anyone could see. The care that
goes into it, the humanity that goes into it,* to see that
military targets are destroyed, to be sure, but that it's
done in a way, and in a manner, and in a direction
and with a weapon that is appropriate to that very
particularized target.[53]

All our mainstream news sources agreed. They did so
explicitly by the endless repetition of stories about how
smart and precise the smart precision weapons were. And
perhaps more importantly, by maintaining a great and
almost total silence about how much human pain and death
would occur even if the weapons were as good as claimed:

it focuses on the psychological destruction of the
enemy's will to fight rather than the physical destruction of his military forces.

"We want them to quit. We want them not to fight,"
says Harlan Ullman, one of the authors of the Shock
and Awe concept which relies on large numbers of precision guided weapons.

'So that you have this simultaneous effect, rather
like the nuclear weapons at Hiroshima, not taking days
or weeks but in minutes," says Ullman.

In the first Gulf War, 10 percent of the weapons were
precision guided. In this war 80 percent will be precision
guided.

The Air Force has stockpiled 6,000 of these guidance

53. www.pbs.org/newshour/bb/middle_east/jan-june03/rumsfeld_3-21.html.

kits in the Persian Gulf to convert ordinary dumb bombs into satellite-guided bombs, a weapon that didn't exist in the first war.

"You're sitting in Baghdad and all of a sudden you're the general and 30 of your division headquarters have been wiped out. You also take the city down. By that I mean you get rid of their power, water. In 2, 3, 4, 5 days they are physically, emotionally and psychologically exhausted," Ullman tells Martin.

Last time, an armored armada swept into Kuwait and destroyed Saddam's elite republican guard divisions in the largest tank battle since the World War II. This time, the target is not the Iraqi army but the Iraqi leadership, and the battle plan is designed to bypass Iraqi divisions whenever possible.

CBS Evening News, January 27, 2003

In spite of the emphasis on how much smarter the bombs are this time than last time, viewers who watched the First Iraq War—and who among us didn't?—might be forgiven for thinking that the bombs back then were really smart already. Downright brilliant. Here is the smart bomb myth from the First Iraq War:

Gen. Horner stepped up to the podium in Riyadh on Jan. 18 to show a bomb hitting the roof of the 13-story Iraqi air force headquarters building. The image would come to symbolize smart war. F-117s [that] could hit "targets as small as a one-yard-wide vent shaft," the media reported. The Air Force gushed that an F-117 pilot on opening night "cruised over Iraqi air force headquarters, dropping a smart bomb down its elevator shaft and blowing out the bottom of the building."

The Gulf War: Secret History, William M. Arkin

The video was replayed so often it became the virtual logo of the First Iraq War. It was repeated over and over. Precision. Never a civilian harmed.

In 1943, back when all bombs where dumb as bricks, RKO Pictures produced a movie called *Bombardier* with Randolph Scott and Pat O'Brian.

The film is set in a training center. A young recruit gets a letter from his mom. His mom doesn't want her son dropping bombs. They might kill civilians. The young man is deeply affected and wants to quit.

Pat sits him down and shows him how, by a miracle of exclusive American technology—the Norton bombsight—an American bombardier can home in on a military target so precisely that he can be sure that he will hit that target and only that target.

Convinced by both the science of it all and by the sincerity of his leaders, the young man goes back into the bombers.

In the final climatic scene, he is in a bomber flying over Japan. There is a munitions factory down below. The chief addresses the young bombardier:

CREW CHIEF
Put one in the smokestack.

AERIAL SHOT, BOMBARDIER'S POV.

It's a large, sprawling complex. The main building has three smokestacks.

                    BOMBARDIER
    Which one?

CUT BACK TO INT. BOMBER.

                    CHIEF
    Center one.

                    BOMBARDIER
    That's easy.

The bombardier looks down through the bombsight. Fixes on the target. Releases the bomb. The bomb goes down toward the building. Right into the middle chimney. It goes down the chimney like Santa Claus and disappears. A beat later there's an explosion from inside the building, and the munitions factory explodes outward.

It's the same scene and almost exactly the same shot we will see fifty-eight years later.

It's there for the same reason. To convince the audience that American bombs do not kill civilians. That audience includes the men who drop the bombs and the men who give the orders. Many, if not most of them, need to believe they are not wantonly killing civilians and preferably that they are not killing civilians at all.

Given that Shock and Awe was explicitly based on the bombing of Hiroshima and Nagasaki, given that this was the largest bombing in history, given that the targets were all in two big cities and one town full of civilians, given that some of these precision munitions went as far afield as Saudi Arabia and Turkey, it ought to be ridiculous that no one seemed to think that there had to be massive civilian casuties.

But no one did.

If there were no WMDs, and if Saddam Hussein had no significant links to Al Qaeda, then the justification for our invasion of Iraq is that we made it a better place. Part of what made it a bad place was that Saddam Hussein killed people. Sure, it's a crude measure, but if we killed more people than he did, civilians in particular, did we make it a better place?

General Tommy Frank was asked about Iraqi casualties. He said "We're don't do body counts." It never seemed to occur to the producers and editors at CBS, CNN, Fox, the *New York Times,* and the *Washington Post* or to the reporters on ground that they should do their own body counts, impelled by logic or curiosity, in search of a story or in search of the truth. Net searches for "Iraqi casualties" showed a single story from the Associated Press, recycled through several venues, that repeated the general's assertion and then went on to say that any estimates of Iraqi casualties would be very difficult to make. They did not make any. And that seemed to be the end of it. There was one exception, a Web site called Iraqbodycount.com, that appeared about six months after the invasion and attempted to track casualties through newspaper accounts. They were very cautious and conservative. After about a year they were up around 12,000.

Finally, in 2004, a research team from Johns Hopkins did the equivalent of an epidemiological study. They went to Iraq and conducted interviews and asked people how many members of their families had died since the war and how many had died during an equivalent period before the invasion:

Iraqis were 2.5 times more likely to die in the 17 months following the invasion than in the 14 months before it. Before the invasion, the most common causes of death in Iraq were heart attacks, strokes and chronic diseases. Afterward, violent death was far ahead of all other causes.

International Herald Tribune, October 30, 2004

Their estimate was that 100,000 civilians had died as a result of the war:

The researchers found that the majority of deaths were attributed to violence, which were primarily the result of military actions by Coalition forces. Most of those killed by Coalition forces were women and children.

John Hopkins School of Public Health
Public Health Center
October 26, 2004

Fog facts.
And a triumph for the Soft Machine.
To create 100,000 corpses and never have them seen.

Chapter Eleven

OUT OF THE FOG

WHY ARE FOG FACTS fog facts?

The nexus is journalism. Reporters go out and gather the news. Then the news media bring it to us. They decide what story will lead, what barely gets a mention, and what isn't covered at all.

Reporters, editors, and producers will tell you that their decisions are based on a mixture of journalistic expertise and market forces. If a story seems to them to be important—it affects the fate of nations, it affects us all, it is traditionally considered notable, it resonates, it's dramatic, it's sexy, it has great visuals—they'll run it. If it attracts viewers and keeps their eyeballs on the screen, they'll keep running it as long as they can find something new about it. When that story runs out, they'll look for something else like it as soon as they can find it.

They check their ratings, they check their sales figures. They are working very, very hard to give us "what we want."

Then how come so many people are dissatisfied with the

news and so many people distrust it? The right wing says it's because of the liberal elite who run the media. The left says it's because the media are being manipulated by corporate interests and intimidated by the right. Those in the media respond that if both left and right are upset, it's because they are doing something correct: telling the truth and making all sides uncomfortable.

When I write a book, I usually give the manuscript to as many people who are willing to read it as I can. After publication, of course, I want nothing but praise. But prepublication, the point is to fix it as much as possible.

What I have come to understand through that process is that if someone says they don't like the book or some part of it—or worse, they don't even finish it, which is the most telling criticism of all—that is an absolute truth. They did not like the book. No amount of arguing, explaining, second-guessing, or justification will change that.

When they go on to tell me why they didn't like the book and how to fix it, then they are almost invariably wrong. There are exceptions. My wife often has astonishing insights. Some friend or other will, in the midst of fifteen minutes of dialogue, make one key observations that makes me say: Yes, that's it.

So far, having read about twelve media criticism books and endless available online essays, I can say that there are only a few bits, here and there, that have made me say: Yes, that's it.

But I am certain that if so many people say something is wrong, then something is wrong.

JOURNALISM 101: OBJECTIVE JOURNALISM

The American journalistic tradition is called objective journalism, in distinction to the European tradition, in which most newspapers were affiliated with a particular political party—conservative, liberal, socialist, communist, royalist—and their coverage was expected to reflect that orientation.

Objective journalists are supposed to report "the facts." They are not supposed to express their own opinions or evaluate, interpret, or frame the facts.

There is a certain purity and integrity and modesty in that. But, as with so many other things in life, its very strengths are its greatest institutional weakness.

The classic way to put together a story that requires interpretation or opinion—and most do—is like ordering a dinner special at a Chinese restaurant: one from column A, one from column B, and occasionally reach out to an expert to get one from column C. This is also called "he said/she said" journalism.

The weakness in this is that it requires two vigorous, reputable sides to make it work.

"Reputable" tends to mean an official government or institutional authority.

Generally, "reputable people" only have very mainstream views. The rules of the game do not allow the media to evaluate things for themselves, so that, too, makes them feel more comfortable.

Here is a quintessential example of how the media treat a situation in which a high-ranking government official says something that is untrue, and the wrong person tells the truth, and, even worse, what he says is outside the mainstream and is going against what everyone else is saying.

On February 5, 2003, Colin Powell gave his famous speech at the United Nations General Assembly in which he offered "proof" that Saddam had WMDs and that there was a "sinister nexus" that linked Al Qaeda and Iraq. Powell had many visual aids. Satellite photos. Videos. Diagrams. A vial of white powder!

> On CNN, after General Amer al-Saadi, Saddam Hussein's scientific adviser, appeared to offer a point-by-point rebuttal of Powell's charges, anchor Paula Zahn brought on former State Department spokesman James Rubin to comment. Introducing Rubin, Zahn said, "You've got to understand that most Americans watching this were either probably laughing out loud or got sick to their stomach. Which was it for you?"
>
> "Well, really, both," Rubin replied. The American people "will believe everything they saw," he said. "They have no reason to doubt any of [Powell's] sources, any of the references to human sources, any of the pictures, or any of the intercepts."

> "Rethinking Objectivity," Brent Cunningham,
> *Columbia Journalism Review,* July/August, 2003

"Objective" journalism is very susceptible to spin.

Spin is more sophisticated than old-fashioned political posturing or propaganda. If it's any good, it does not involve specific, outright lies.

> Facing clear evidence of peril, we cannot wait for the final proof—the smoking gun—that could come in the form of a mushroom cloud.

> George Bush, Cincinnati, Ohio, October 7, 2002

That's a true statement. It is also an entirely misleading one. "Facing clear evidence of peril" is a conditional phrase. If we were in that situation, it might be true that we could not wait for "the final proof," especially if Saddam Hussein had nukes and the means to deliver them. Neither of which he had.

What is a journalist to do with that? Call in a linguistics expert and present a dissection of the nonstatement statement that creates a state of fear and a justification for invasion?

When both sides are spinning, spinning as hard as they can, and the media gives us both spins, it doesn't really help either. We know that neither side is being forthright and accurate, and we either say: A plague on both your houses; or choose the side we liked in the first place and blame the messenger for not having sorted it out.

Fog facts remain fog facts because no one has made an effective effort to make them otherwise.

With certain obvious exceptions—tsunamis, dead popes, elections, invasions, and the like—facts do not declare themselves. A significant portion of the facts that appear in the media are born as a press release. Even in humble and innocent ways. The Little League schedule does not get into your local paper by itself. The coach's wife Xeroxes it and mails it in.

> A study by Scott Cutlip, ex-dean of the School of Journalism and Mass Communications at the University of Georgia, found that forty percent of the news content in a typical U.S. newspaper originated with public relations press releases, story memos, or suggestions.
>
> *Unreliable Sources: A Guide to Detecting Bias in News Media,* Martin A. Lee and Norman Solomon
> (Lyle Stuart, 1990)

In 1980 the Columbia Journalism Review scrutinized a typical issue of the *Wall Street Journal* and found that more than half of its news stories "were based solely on releases." Often the releases were reprinted "almost verbatim or in paraphrase," ... "Most of what you see on TV is, in effect, a canned PR product. Most of what you read in the paper and see on television is not news," says the senior vice president of a leading public relations firm.

> *Trust Us, We're Experts,* Sheldon Rampton and
> John Stauber (Penguin Putnam, 2002)

PUBLIC RELATIONS 101

Public Relations is new. It was born with the twentieth century. America's first PR firm, the Publicity Bureau, was founded in Boston in 1900. The first famous PR man was Ivy Ledbetter Lee.

Fraser Seitel, author of *The Practice of Public Relations,* wrote:

> Lee, more than anyone before him, lifted the field from a questionable pursuit (that is, seeking positive publicity at any cost) to a professional discipline designed to win public confidence and trust through communications based on candor and truth."

Part of the way Lee did that was with his Declaration of Principles. Its summary paragraph is:

> In brief, our plan is, frankly and openly, on behalf of

business concerns and public institutions, to supply the press and public of the United States prompt and accurate information concerning subjects which it is of value and interest to the public to know about.

It is important to see how that works in practice. The case on which Lee made his reputation is an instructive example: guiding the media response of the Rockefellers after the Ludlow Massacre.

Coal miners had gone out on strike against Colorado Fuel & Iron, a Rockefeller company, in September 1913. The company owned the shacks the miners lived in, so they evicted them. Indeed, the company owned all the housing in the area, so the miners set up a tent city. Rockefeller's company hired the Baldwin–Felts Detective Agency to help break the strike. These were not the kind of detectives that Warner Brothers made Humphrey Bogart movies about. They were skull-breakers and enforcers, used mostly by big companies against unions. In Ludlow they had an armored car with a machine gun mounted on it. They called it the "Death Special," and they would drive it around and fire randomly into the camp where the miners lived with their wives and children.

In October, the governor called in the National Guard to back up Rockefeller's private army.

Nonetheless, the miners and their families survived through the hard Colorado winter and into the spring.

On April 14, 1914, the National Guard, along with the security people, began firing into the camp with machine guns. The miners fought back. The battle raged through the day. When night came, the Guard attacked and burned the camp:

The Ludlow camp is a mass of charred debris, and buried beneath it is a story of horror unparalleled in the history of industrial warfare. In the holes which had been dug for their protection against the rifles' fire the women and children died like trapped rats when the flames swept over them. One pit, uncovered [after the massacre] disclosed the bodies of ten children and two women.

New York Times, April 21, 1914

Lee put out bulletins that claimed that the miners provoked the attack, that the fire that killed the two women and ten children was caused by an overturned stove, and that Mother Jones, one of the heroines of the strike, ran a whorehouse. Lee also had Rockefeller go to Ludlow and speak to the miners man to man: "We are all partners. . . . Capital can't get along without you men, and you men can't get along without capital."

Then he helped the Rockefellers invent company unions. These were front organizations run by the companies to keep real unions out. They were outlawed in 1935 by the Wagner Act.

In sum, the man so admired for making public relations reputable and ethical, for bringing candor and professionalism to the business, helped a giant corporation avoid the consequences of the multiple murders that had been committed on its behalf. He did so by telling lies, slandering the victims, and creating a fake organization—the company union—whose actions would be to effect the opposite of what its name promised.

Then, when Hitler came to power and began the persecution of the Jews, Lee went to work for I. G. Farben, the

German chemical giant, to help them keep doing business in the United States as Germany geared up for war

The other founding father of PR is Edward Bernays, the nephew, as he was quick to tell his clients, of Sigmund Freud. Bernays helped Woodrow Wilson convince the American public to enter the First World War. In his book *Propaganda,* he wrote:

> Those who manipulate the unseen mechanisms of society constitute an invisible government which is the true ruling power. We are governed, our minds molded, our tastes formed, our ideas suggested largely by men we have never heard of . . . whether in the sphere of politics or business, in our social conduct or our ethical thinking, we are dominated by the relatively small number of persons who understand the mental processes and social patterns of the masses. It is they who pull the wires that control the public mind.

Advertising sells us things. It may contain information, but we are put on notice that its intent is to sell us something. That allows us to filter it. Actually, in my house, before I get a chance to ignore it, one of the kids has grabbed the remote and changed the channel.

Public relations tries to sell us something under the guise of offering us information.

If the source is a corporation or a political party or a politician in campaign mode, we know that whatever they are saying could well be skewed by their profit motive or some other interest. Good public relations, therefore, tries to arrange for the real source, which is paying for the story, to fade into the woodwork. It should appear to originate from a third party.

Academic studies have credibility because academics are supposed to produce disinterested scholarship with peer-review standards. The problem is that sometimes they actually do tell the truth and where's the profit in that? The solution is to have "institutes" and "foundations" which sound like places of real study and to give the employees academic titles: like "scholar" and "fellow." Reporters will quote them and op ed pages will print their pieces without ever saying they are the paid spokesmen of special interest groups and political parties.

For certain kinds of information, we turn to the government. They are supposed to be truthful and accurate and yet they are often political. There is a certain irreducible confusion.

For example, presidential press secretary Scott McClellan is a public employee. His job is to facilitate the flow of information about the executive branch from the White House, through the media, to us, the people. Yet he is relentlessly on message and wont let a word slip that won't advance the president and his policies. He is acting, in fact, as PR person. At the same time, he remains the official spokesperson and the gatekeeper for information. No matter how cynical the reporters and the public become about him, it is impossible not to treat what he says as news. He is typical of an administration that has taken spin to new heights:

> George W. Bush . . . has developed a communications strategy of unprecedented scope and sophistication borrowed from the world of public relations. These include emotional language designed to provoke gut-level

reactions, slanted statistics that are difficult for casual listeners to interpret, and ambiguous statements that imply what Bush does not want to state outright. In his continual use of these tactics to mislead the public about his policies, Bush has escalated the war for public opinion, giving birth to what could be called a permanent campaign of policy disinformation.

> *All the President's Spin: George W. Bush, the Media and the Truth,* Ben Fritz, Bryan Keefer, and Brendan Nyhan (Simon & Schuster, 2004)

LEFT AND RIGHT

The right has claimed for years and continues to claim that the mainstream media are dominated by a liberal elite.

The *New York Times* is always picked out as the flagship of that elite.

The *New York Times* went after Bill Clinton and Whitewater relentlessly. To my mind, in 2000 it treated George Bush better than it did Al Gore, and certainly as well as it treated John Kerry in 2004. After 9/11, the *New York Times* participated in the creation of the myth of an articulate, heroic Bush who grew instantly into the stature of his office. It spun the Florida recount story so we would believe Bush was not an illegitimate monarch. It never questioned the invasion of Afghanistan. It put its stamp of approval on the WMD stories and never questioned that Saddam had to go or that we had a right to invade a sovereign country on suspicion of what they might do someday, somewhere down the line.

It is true that the *Times* has, in early 2005, gone after Mr.

Bush on its editorial pages. But that is less a symptom of liberalism than of a genuine conservatism—not the reckless neocon variety:

> The Right had spent so many years castigating the *New York Times* as the flagship of the liberal media that everyone believed it, including the Left, including the people at the *Times* themselves. But the truth was that the *Times* was the house organ of the Establishment. It was committed, both editorially and in its presentation of the news, to the interests of an Establishment: continuity, security and legitimacy. Therefore they generally supported business and finance, the American version of empire, the government and the president, until, and unless, some excess was so egregious that it posed a threat to continuity, security or legitimacy. Then the *Times* would turn on the destabilizers, as they did, at last, on the Vietnam War, on Nixon and on Enron, in the interests of restoring continuity, security and legitimacy.

The Librarian

In spring 2005, with the dollar in free fall, deficits mounting, the economy still flat, and Bush pushing policies that are more of the same, they have begun to panic. That's why they've begun to turn against him. But only on the editorial page. It doesn't show in the news pages.

The right hates CBS and Dan Rather with a particular passion. Why? Dan Rather is the man who said during the run-up to the war in Iraq: "George Bush is the president, he makes the decisions and, you know, as just one American,

[if] he wants me to line up, just tell me where." If that's what a liberal does, what does a right-winger do?

The critique of the media from the left, aside from complaining that the right has too much influence, is that corporations have taken over news organizations, and their concern for the bottom line has debased the product, news.

The dissatisfaction with the media is huge. It was also universal, left and right:

> A recent report from the Pew Research Center, "Trends 2005," is painful to read. The report says that 45 percent of Americans believe little or nothing in their daily newspapers, up from 16 percent two decades ago.
>
> Nicholas Kristof, *New York Times* op-ed column,
> April 11, 2005

The percentage of people who distrust TV news is "only" 35 to 37 percent. But that's still a frightening number if, as the Pew report says, "Trust is the lifeblood of the media's relationship with the people."

The classical economic argument—the Smithian argument—is that if people don't like the product, they won't buy it. Someone will come up with a better product and they'll buy that instead.

But the paradox is that the news media is making money. A ton of money.

Gannett is the largest of the four big newspaper chains. In 2003, according to their annual report, they had net sales of $6.7 billion dollars, a gross profit of $3.3 billion, and a net income of 1.2 billion dollars. That's a gross profit of 48 percent. Their after-tax net profit was 18 percent.

Newspapers generally make 20 to 40 percent profit.

As a point of reference, supermarkets operate on a 2 to 4 percent margin.

Television news makes even more money than print:

> during a panel discussion among television journalists in November 1999 . . . a participant mentioned the estimate that local stations typically make 40 percent profit margins. Long offered a correction. "I guarantee you that 60 to 70 percent is not uncommon in major markets. We make a ton of money. You can't make that kind of money legally in any other way."

> *The News About the News: American Journalism in Peril,* Leonard Downie Jr. and Robert G. Kaiser
> (Knopf, 2002)

According to the Radio and Television News Directors Association, the news produces 40 percent of the revenue of local TV stations.

The best explanation for this phenomenon—companies getting rich from dissatisfied customers—comes from an independent documentary that has nothing to do with media—except the fact that the mainstream media did not make it. It was called *Supersize Me*. The director, Morgan Spurlock ate nothing but McDonald's food for thirty days without exercising and filmed what happened to him.

He put on twenty-five pounds and suffered mood swings, cravings, depression, and the diminishment of his sexual performance, if not total impotence. His cholesterol level went from 165 to 230.

By the twenty-first day, the doctors who were auditing his progress told him to stop. They were afraid that he would have a heart attack and that he was doing as much damage to his liver as an alcoholic after many years of drinking. One of the doctors described his liver as "pickled."

There were three doctors in the film. All of them were astonished at how much damage Spurlock had done to himself and at how quickly it happened. For years, there has been plenty of talk and plenty of articles and plenty of comments on health shows on TV and radio about how eating good food and getting enough exercise are the most important things we can do for our health. Yet the doctors really didn't believe it until they watched a man go from perfect health to a life-threatening condition just by eating the most popular food in America for three weeks.

Here are some fun facts—fog facts—from the film's Web site:

- Sixty percent of all Americans are either overweight or obese.
- Left unabated, obesity will surpass smoking as the leading cause of preventable death in America.
- Only seven items on McDonald's entire menu contain no sugar.
- One in every three children born in the year 2000 will develop diabetes in their lifetime.
- Diabetes cuts 17 to 27 years off a diabetic's life.

In short, a diet of McDonald's food will make you fat and ugly and then kill you. Yet in 2000, McDonald's total sales were over $40 billion.

If we ate for health and nutrition, McDonald's would have gone out of business years ago.

We are evolved creatures. Not rational ones. Had we waited for the science of nutrition to come along and tell us what to eat, our species would have starved to death long before we had our first decent meal. Instead, what we did was develop a taste for certain flavors and textures that are frequently found in nature and go with things that are nutritious.

Some of the primary ones are the flavors of fat and salt and sweetness. When we go to eat, we go to have those buttons pushed, under the unspoken assumption that if we do that, then nutrition will ensue.

Our actual diet is always modified by our culture and by the lessons of experience. The application of rationality can make it more healthful and nutritious.

But the opposite can also happen.

Rationality can be applied to maximizing the button pushing and cutting the costs. So McDonald's offers fat and salt and high-fructose corn syrup along with other flavors that extensive testing has proved that we are responsive. If the food that goes with those button pushers does not have a great deal of nutrition, indeed, even if it kills you (in a manner that does not incur civil or criminal liability), that's not McDonald's business. That's yours.

Commercial news, especially television news, is to real news what McDonald's is to food.

We respond to threats, excitement, glitz, celebrity, and attractive people. We respond to the promise of things to be revealed ("This! Up next!"), to relevance to ourselves ("Stay tuned to find out what it means to *you!*"), and to reinforcement of our beliefs.

As with fast food, where the buttons do not have to be attached to valuable nutrition, with fast-food news, the buttons do not need to be attached to important or even true information. Real news requires real money and may not result in good pictures, sexy headlines, or tantalizing teasers.

In a true business environment, fast-food news is the only way to go. Anything else is fiscally irresponsible.

The exceptions prove the rule. The exceptions are all family owned (or at least controlled) —the *New York Times*, the *Washington Post*, and (until quite recently) the *L.A. Times*—or quasi public—NPR, PBS, the BBC.

THE VAST RIGHT-WING CONSPIRACY

I believe in the vast right-wing conspiracy because four of the conspirators told me about it.

They have not pulled me aside and whispered their secrets to me. As with everything else discussed in this book, information about it is quite public.

Back in 1980, Terry Dolan, chairman of the National Conservative Political Action Committee, in an interview with the *Washington Post,* said:

> Groups like ours are potentially very dangerous to the political process. We could be a menace, yes. . . . We could say whatever we want about an opponent of a Senator Smith and the senator would not have to say anything. A group like ours could lie through its teeth and the candidate it helps stays clean.

In 2002, David Brock, the author of *Blinded by the Right:*

The Conscience of an Ex-Conservative revealed what one reviewer (Tim Apello, Amazon.com) called "a ghastly right-wing Clinton-bashing conspiracy of hypocrites, zillionaires, and maniacs; [Brock] accuses himself of being 'a witting cog in the Republican sleaze machine.'" That was followed by Brock's *The Republican Noise Machine: The Right-Wing Media and How It Corrupts Democracy* (Crown, 2004). It details how the right has funded scholarships, training programs, ideological think tanks, newspapers, and publishers and how they will all work together to create heavily spun or downright false stories, which they then repeat to each other until those stories make their way into the mainstream media and become part of a manufactured reality.

The other two are Richard A. Viguerie and David Franke, the authors of *America's Right Turn: How Conservatives Used New and Alternative Media to Take Power*. Viguerie should be well known to all political junkies. He practically invented political direct mail and, according to the jacket copy, "The *AFL-CIO News* said Viguerie 'made it all possible' for conservatives and the *Washington Post* has called him 'the conservatives' Voice of America.'" The book is a cheerful boast about how he did it.

Chapter 1 is called "The Media Revolution of 1517." Any book that starts out by explaining how Martin Luther beat the Vatican using the new media of the day, the printed pamphlet, is a smart and aware piece of work.

Then they offer their "Recipe for Creating a New Mass Movement." Liberals, Democrats, progressives, people on the left or even in the middle should all take note. The ingredient list is:

1. Issues that motivate
2. A dedicated vanguard
3. Self-identification as a movement
4. Communication networks
5. Money to fund the revolution
6. And then there's the establishment . . .

Conservatives, they explain, had it much worse than the liberals do now. They were once a real minority party, a fringe movement, ignored, neglected, and abused. Here's the portrait they draw of what to them were the bad old days of complete liberal hegemony:

> In 1955, liberalism reigned supreme over the politics of the United States. . . . The slant of TV news and commentary was solidly liberal, without exception. . . . Influential newspapers were virtually all liberal, too. . . . Liberals controlled the academy as tightly as they controlled the TV networks. . . . The foundation world was dominated by liberal giants. . . . All the major book publishers were liberal. . . .
>
> Put together all the influential media and you get a score of something like liberals 95, conservatives 5. Or perhaps it was more like 97/3. That's the sort of monopoly enjoyed by *Pravda* in its Soviet heydey.

These guys are good writers and excellent persuaders. And if I hadn't been there—in America in the fifties and sixties—and stopped to think about it now, I would have believed them.

Emmett Till was lynched in 1955. He had whistled at a white woman. He was fourteen.

America was a segregated country. Although those damn "activist judges" on the Supreme Court had ruled in 1954 that "Separate educational facilities are inherently unequal," and public schools could not be segregated, the change had not yet taken place. The ruling applied only to schools. Not to the rest of the Jim Crow system, which remained in effect in the South by law and in the North by custom.

It was illegal in many states for a white person to marry a black person. The damn activist judges would not rule such antimiscegenation laws unconstitutional until 1967. The Alabama law was not repealed until 2000.

In 1955 the Supreme Court refused to rule on a state law that forbade a Jewish couple from adopting Catholic twins.

Women knew their place. It helped that if they had sex they were likely to get pregnant. In many states it was illegal for a doctor to tell even a married couple about contraception. That would not change until 1965. Of course, abortion was illegal until 1973. Network codes forbade the use of the word "pregnant" in TV shows. Bedrooms on television had separate beds.

Domestic violence was socially acceptable. Standard American police procedure was not to make arrests in such cases.

Homosexuality was, of course, illegal. It would remain so until 2003. Though in those days people went to prison for it. People also went to prison for publishing books about sex.

There was a draft.

The Pledge of Allegiance was written in 1892: "And to the Republic for which it stands, one nation with liberty and justice for all." It wasn't until 1954 that the words "under God" were added.

There was a Republican president. (Real conservatives consider Eisenhower to have been a liberal. Hardcores consider him to have been a "crypto-socialist" who let the Russkies take Berlin. Robert Welch, the founder of the John Birch Society, wrote in his book, *The Politician*, that Ike was "a dedicated conscious agent of the communist conspiracy.") People were being fired and blacklisted for their political opinions and for refusing to testify about the political activities of their friends and neighbors.

Viguerie and Franke think those were the bad old days when liberal hegemony was absolute? They think 1955 was not conservative enough? And they are fighting to get to the right of that?

The Vast Left-Wing Dishevelment

In the final decades of the twentieth century—from Reagan to Bush I to Clinton through the start of Bush II—it seemed as if most of America's serious political differences had melted away. The Soviet Union had collapsed. National security and being tough on communism were nonissues. Clinton was tough on crime and for welfare reform. He was not only probusiness, he was so much better at the economy than the Republicans that they could not claim to out-capitalist him either.

Sex was the only issue that divided the parties. Abortion (which is about whether there are consequences for having sex), gay rights, gays in the military, welfare (which is mostly aid to dependent children, that is, consequences for having sex), were among the few issues in contention in the Clinton-versus-Dole campaign. The Gore-versus-Bush campaign was a New Democrat with Rectitude versus a Compassionate Conservative with Moral Values, ideologically indistinguishable people, both of them running against Clinton's sexuality, so even sex had become a consensus issue. At least in terms of the official public dialogue.

Until 9/11, Bush bumbled along with bad ideas that weren't bearing fruit but that had not yet created a lot of damage. The neoconservatives, the financial radicals, and the Christian fundamentalists may have been coming out of the closet, but they were not yet in charge.

As President Bush likes to say—again and again and again and again—9/11 changed everything.

Bush actually reacted very ineptly to the events of 9/11.

The media protected him. "The media" is, after all, a conglomeration of individuals. Many of them live in New York. They were filled with panic. And with the tribal instinct that is deeper even than patriotism to band together in the face of attack.

Bush froze when he heard about the attacks on the World Trade Center. But it would be three years before someone showed us the footage, which had been available all along, of his vacant face as he sat in a kindergarten chair reading *My Pet Goat*.

I was in born in New York. I spent most of my life there, though I live upstate now. I expected that the president would go to the scene of the disaster. Or perhaps to Washington to figuratively take the helm of the ship of state. Instead he flew as far from any possible target as he could. New York was burning, the Pentagon had been hit, the country was in a panic; George Bush went to Nebraska.

There was no outcry from the media.

It took him three days to get to New York. When he did

and he got a photo op and made a rousing speech, the media did not ask why it took so long or ask him where he had been. They were so relieved that he was making patriotic noises that they turned themselves into a Greek chorus singing paeans, as if he was a hero out of Homer.

Bush understood, from watching his father, the power of leading in "wartime." It makes the public malleable, leaves the opposition tongue-tied, and turns the press into a pep squad. He seized the moment and hastened, against real reason, to make himself a "war president." It worked, as he knew it would and those who misunderestimated him did not, which is why he speaks of it with such glee.

He himself has said that by doing so, he accumulated political capital. He proceeded to use it. He also got a very right-wing, very activist Republican Congress and, by a hair, a Republican Senate. The conservative movement had been around for a long time. But right up through 9/11, they still appeared to be a radical fringe group. They ranted about tearing down the New Deal, returning to laissez-faire capitalism, and making America a Christian nation. Nobody thought that the president and the leaders of the Republican Party would take up their cause and make a serious attempt actually to do those things.

They caught everyone—the Democrats, the left, the mainstream, the media, and even old-fashioned Republicans—asleep.

Self-respecting journalists expect to act like honest brokers, right-wing and left-wing radio and certain talk shows and Fox News excepted.

What they want is strong statements from both sides. As Steven Weisman pointed out, when they get strong statements from only one side, they do not know how to make up the deficit. If another side does not speak up, journalists in a sense do not "know" there is another side.

When the media gets pressure from only one side, they will yield to that pressure.

The left and the mainstream have fought many battles since the fifties.

While they are full of interest groups, from the Sierra Club to the NAACP to NOW, they have not invested in anything like what David Brock calls the Republican Noise Machine: a loose but interlocked association of a political party with youth recruitment, scholarships, fellowships, think tanks, publishers, newspapers, and a television network.

This is in part because so much of what the right calls liberal and the liberals would consider mainstream has proven itself and it seems self-explanatory. Equal rights are good. Anybody should be able to study any subject and enter any field. Adults should be able to have sex with whom they want, avoid diseases, and control when they have children. Universal education and access to higher education are good. The success and the simple utility of Social Security, the FDIC, the Securities and Exchange Commission, keeping an eye on the banks, all seem self-evident. Clean air and clean water and keeping vanishing species alive all seem like sound ideas. That science is a better basis for biology than prayer is a choice we make every time we visit the doctor or take an aspirin.

But it has abruptly emerged that there are a lot of people to whom these ideas are not, in fact, self-evident. That means if we, in the mainstream, in the reality-based community, care about those ideas, we have to put in the effort to explain them and justify them and then to proselytize. The idea of proselytizing practicality, realism, and objectivity sounds strange, but in a world of theologians it becomes necessary.

The Pew report that so upset Nicholas Kristof was called *Trends 2005: The Media, More Choices, Less Credibility.* In addition to the general disenchantment with the mainstream media, the survey revealed a split between Republicans and Democrats.

Whereas 45 percent of Democrats believed all or most of what they heard on CNN, only 26 percent of Republicans did; 35 percent of Democrats trusted CBS, 15 percent of Republicans. And so on, right down the line, a little more than twice as many Democrats as Republicans believed in the major media.

This held true even for the AP and for C-SPAN, which are about as neutral as it's possible to get and still report straight news.

The only places the gap was less was with Fox and the *Wall Street Journal.* But that was because the numbers went down for the Democrats. Only 29 percent of Republicans believed what they saw on Fox, not much higher than the 26 percent that trusted CNN or the 25 percent that trusted *60 Minutes.* Republicans even mistrusted the *Wall Street Journal.* Only 23 percent gave it credibility, compared to 29 percent of Democrats.

I would like to suggest that the split is not between right and left but between the faith-based and reality-based communities.

When the right attacks the liberal media, what it is really attacking is objective media, with fact-checking.

There have been two surprise success stories in the news business in recent years. The first and most obvious one is Fox News.

The conventional analysis, and Fox's own analysis, is that their popularity is a result of providing a healthy and much desired righteous right-wing antidote to the whiny pap of the liberal hegemony. If we put aside the political orientation, it becomes clear that Fox is performing a service for their customers that the rest of the mainstream television news media is not. They put the news in context. They give it a perspective. They tell the viewer, this is how to think about the stories. Even if they're wrong, for many of their viewers it is still more satisfying than the conventional, non-judgmental approach that leaves the audience with work to do.

It is possible to offer perspective and to put things in context, while still being objective and without necessarily putting a partisan spin on the information.

For instance, the administration said it was going base the occupation of Iraq on the successful occupations of Germany and Japan. They were going into Iraq with about 150,000 men and women and talking about getting out quickly. A quick net search would have discovered that the occupations of Germany and Japan were far more massive:

On V-E Day, Eisenhower had sixty-one U.S. divisions, 1,622,000 men, in Germany, and a total force in Europe numbering 3,077,000. When the shooting ended, the divisions in the field became the occupation troops, charged with maintaining law and order and establishing the Allied military presence in the defeated nation. This was the army-type occupation. . . .

The army-type occupation was comprehensive and showed the Germans that they were defeated and their country occupied. This type of occupation was presumably capable of squelching incipient resistance since none was evident.

> *The U.S. Army in the Occupation of Germany: 1944-1946,*
> Army Historical Series, Earl F. Ziemke
> Center of Military History, United States Army,
> Washington, D.C., 1990

Germany was run by the military occupation until 1949.

General MacArthur occupied Japan with about 350,000 Americans, plus 40,000 British Commonwealth troops. The country was devastated. The Japanese were completely dependent on the occupying army for everything, food, fuel, water, medicine and sanitation.

It's been sixty years. US troops are still in both Germany and Japan. It's fifty years since the Korean War and our troops are still there too.

There was another reason the occupations met little resistance. Japan had been at war since the invasion of Manchuria in 1931, Germany since 1939. By the time they surrendered both countries were pulling kids out of middle school and handing guns to sixty years olds.

It's young men who throw rocks, pick up guns and fight for their country. By the end of World War II, all the young men of Germany and Japan were wounded or crippled. The quick war against Saddam Hussein left the youth of Iraq intact.

Germany and Japan were both ethnically and religiously homogeneous.

There is a much better model at hand for what happens when the iron hand of a dictator is removed from such a country: Yugoslavia. After Tito the country devolved into civil war, separatism, chaos, murder, rape, ethnic cleansing and the need for outside intervention.

The mainstream media could have added all the above information to the discussion of the Iraqi occupation without being partisan and without the fear of being called unpatriotic.

The other surprise success in the news market is *The Daily Show.* It's supposed to be a comedy show. Lots of people watch it instead of the "regular" news:

> *Daily Show* viewers know more about election issues than people who regularly read newspapers or watch television news, according to the National Annenberg Election Survey.

> CNN, September 29, 2004

Here is an example of why people who watch *The Daily Show* are better informed than people who watch CNN. In 2005, Paul Wolfowitz was named to head the World Bank. The World Bank's function is to help Third World countries with their economies. *The Daily Show* ran clips of Wolfowitz testifying before Congress about the Iraq War. He predicted with great certainty that Iraq's oil revenue would pay for its reconstruction. Then he said that it was inconceivable that it would take more troops to pacify Iraq than to conquer it. It was a very graphic demonstration that Wolfowitz's judgment about economics and his understanding of the Third World were both about as wrong as it is possible to be.

That was the real "news" about the appointment. And that was exactly what the mainstream media failed to tell us.

Framing. Context. Accountability.

These lead to the really big step. Making judgments. Going beyond he said/she said and letting the reader sort it out, to making objective judgments because there is, frequently, objective truth.

One of the most disturbing trends in the years since 9/11 is that there no longer seem to be any consequences for political lying. The secret Downing Street memo, secret and strictly personal, revealed—at the very least—that the head of British intelligence had been informed by his Washington counterparts that the White House was cooking the books on the information that they use to create a war in Iraq. It was not considered news by the establishment media in the U.S. Byron Calame, the incoming public editor at the *New York Times*, asked Phil Taubman, the *Times*'s Washington bureau chief, why. Taubman emailed him back that "Given what has been reported about war planning in Washington, the revelations about the Downing Street memo did not seem like a bolt from the blue." In other words, everyone in Washington and in the news business already knew that the administration had lied repeatedly. What the people inside the media don't understand is that they had not told us that the administration had knowingly cooked the books.

The failure of the media to take responsibility is the reason that political lying—especially in the soft-core, public relations style that misleads—has no penalties anymore.

Part of the problem is that there is disconnect between what the media does and the effect that it has. That's what fog facts are. All the things in this book have been reported. Yet many of them remain unknown and those that are known have only crept up on us over several years as the consequences of their being unknown have emerged and asserted themselves as—for example—the ever increasing body count in Iraq and the increasing number of terrorist incidents world-wide.

Mainstream journalism is capable of taking those responsibilities, telling us when someone is lying or misleading, giving us context and giving prominence to important news. It requires reporters and editors to make their own objective judgments. There are dangers in that. But there is a model in place for how to do it. It has now become normal to go through political advertising line-by-line and dare to make objective assessments of what is true and what is false, of what is partially true, and even of what is distorted, and to say so. This isn't done by cutting and pasting quotes from the opposing sides. Reporters do their own fact-checking and announce their judgments.

The same thing can be done to any news story that requires it.

The American tradition is a pragmatic one. If it works, we'll do it. That's where the mainstream is. It's neither right nor left. It's certainly not socialist. But neither do we want the Enrons, Halliburtons, and Harkens to run free, pillaging and looting and leaving other people to hold their bankrupt bags. It's strong on defense, but we believe in wars that are necessary, waged in ways that make sense. We believe in letting people believe however they want. We believe in keeping religion out of government, because once it gets into government, we know that it won't let somebody believe the way they want. We believe in innocent until proven guilty and we believe in getting the bad guys and putting them away. We want open government so we can judge ourselves what's going on. The men and women we elect to office running the place because there has to be division of labor, not because they know better than we do.

This is a practical issue. Not merely a moral one. If you drive around in the fog, you must go very slowly. Americans like to go fast. When you speed in the fog, eventually you crash into something.

ACKNOWLEDGMENTS

CARL BROMLEY, THE editorial director of Nation Books suggested this book to me. I thank him for the opportunity and for his support. He is the best of editors.

I also want to thank Ruth Baldwin, the associate editor who turns efficiency into just another manifestation of her charm.

Bonnie Nadel brought me to Nation Books, the most likable publishing house I've met. With the best parties. It's a co-venture of The Nation Institute and Avalon Publishing Group which has brought me into contact with several other marvelous people, Hamilton Fish, Michele Martin, and John Oakes.

I need to mention Linda Kosarin, the art director. This is my third book with Nation Books, after *The Librarian* and *Wag the Dog* and they all had incredibly good covers and been well laid out inside as well.

Several people read the manuscript as it went. My wife, Gillian Farrell, first and foremost, with dedication beyond the call of duty.

John Dean read it, apparently in forty-five minutes, the instant I sent it to him, and told me everything that was wrong with it. I thought long and hard about what he said and I think it led to a much-improved book.

Moses Silverman made quite a few useful suggestions. He disagreed with some points in the book. Responding to them made the book stronger.

Spencer Rumsey of *Newsday* was kind enough to read it and offered his support as well as his insights.

Dr. Justin Frank offered me his thoughts about the psychology of it all, in addition to what is in his fine book, *Bush on the Couch.*

During the period that led up to the creation of the book, I was involved with a public access TV show, *In Your Face,* that made it out into the world over satellite on Free Speech TV. I worked with a bunch of people there who were always sharing political thoughts and ideas and information with me. Most prominent among them were Richard Fusco and Jeff Moran, who also read the manuscript for me.

Robert Brill of the *Albany Times Union,* Clarence Page of the *Chicago Tribune,* and Greg Mitchell of *Editor and Publisher* all were kind enough to speak to me on the record. Though in Rob's case, neither of us knew it at the time. There were several people in the news business who do not want to be named, and they shall not be.

If I have forgotten anyone, please forgive me, Carl Bromley only gave me three months to write the thing and this is the last day.

INDEX

The subject of this book is ongoing.
As I write it, things are changing and I want to add and subtract. Fortunately, we are in the age of the Internet and books need not end when they end.

To continue this dialog go to:

FOGFACTS.COM

To contact the author:

beinhart@fogfacts.com